Swimming	Donald L. Gambril *California State College at Long Beach*
Fundamentals of Physical Education	J. Tillman Hall *University of Southern California* Kenneth C. Lersten *University of Southern California* Merrill J. Melnick *University of Southern California* Talmage W. Morash *San Fernando Valley State College* Richard H. Perry *University of Southern California* Robert A. Pestolesi *California State College at Long Beach* Burton Seidler *California State College at Los Angeles*
Volleyball	Randy Sandefur *California State College at Long Beach*
Tennis	Barry C. Pelton *University of Houston*
Women's Basketball	Ann Stutts *San Fernando Valley State College*
Women's Gymnastics	Mary L. Schreiber *California State College at Los Angeles*

GOODYEAR PUBLISHING COMPANY, INC.
Pacific Palisades, California 90272

HANDBALL

GOODYEAR
Physical Activities Series

Edited by J. Tillman Hall

Archery Jean A. Barrett
*California State College
at Fullerton*

Badminton James Poole
Tulane University

Bowling Norman E. Showers
Southern Illinois University

Fencing Nancy L. Curry
Southwest Missouri State College

Folk Dance J. Tillman Hall
University of Southern California

Golf Edward F. Chui
University of Hawaii

Handball Pete Tyson
University of Texas

Men's Basketball Richard H. Perry
University of Southern California

Men's Gymnastics Gordon Maddux
*California State College
at Los Angeles*

Soccer John Callaghan
University of Southern California

Social Dance John G. Youmans
Temple University

Goodyear Physical Activities Series

J. Tillman Hall: *Series Editor*

Pete Tyson

University of Texas

HANDBALL

Acknowledgments

I wish to thank the United States Handball Association for their permission to reprint the USHA Rules and for providing several photographs for this book. My thanks also to Mr. Don Bushore of the Athletic Institute for providing and allowing the use of a number of photographs, and to the players whose pictures appear in this book: Jeff Barnes, Howie Eisenberg, Paul Haber, Dennis Hofflander, Jimmy Jacobs, Oscar Obert, Ruby Obert, Steve Sandler and Gary Wiede. Special appreciation is expressed to Mr. Ed Barlow for his guidance, to Cynthia Orlin and my wife, Vyrla Dean, for typing the manuscript, and to Clyde Bennett for his photography.

HANDBALL
Pete Tyson

© Copyright 1971 by
GOODYEAR PUBLISHING COMPANY, INC.
Pacific Palisades, California

Library of Congress Catalog Card Number: 73-141160

ISBN: 0-87620-375-6   (p)
ISBN: 0-87620-376-4   (c)

Y3756-7   (p)   Y3764-1 (c)

Current printing (last number):
10   9   8   7   6   5   4   3

Printed in the United States of America

Editor's note

The Goodyear Publishing Company presents a series of physical education books written by instructor's expert in their respective fields.

These books on major sports are intended as supplementary material for the instructor and to aid the student in the understanding and mastery of his chosen sport. Each book covers the fundamentals— the beginning techniques, rules and customs, equipment, and terms—and gives to the reader the spirit of the sport.

Each author of this series brings to the reader the knowledge and skill he has acquired over many years of teaching and coaching. We sincerely hope these books will prove invaluable to any student of the sport.

In HANDBALL, Pete Tyson supplies everything the beginning player should know about this furious game. He then goes on to present the strategy and techniques for the advanced player and tournament competitor. With 80 photographs, many sequential, and 45 line illustrations, Professor Tyson clearly depicts the correct form used in the execution of *all* of the various shots and serves—including proper height and angles.

Professor Tyson, himself a past handball champion and coach of the nation's leading handball team, here presents the strategies of singles and doubles play, an outlined step-by-step program for the beginning player, and practice methods used to best learn the various offensive and defensive shots. His book presents the challenge, fun, and excitement of this furiously paced game.

Contents

History

Handball may be the oldest of all games played with a ball. Records indicate that the game was played in Ireland as early as the eleventh century. The name handball appeared in Egyptian and Greek literature long before the eleventh century, but there is no way of knowing whether the references were to a contest like the one we call handball. Games similar to handball were played over two hundred years ago in several European countries. In France the game was called *Jeu de Paume*, and in Spain it was referred to as *Pelota*. We know little about these games but think that they were brought to Europe by the early Roman conquerors.

We know more about the game called "Fives"—so called because of the five fingers on a hand—played in England during the seventeenth, eighteenth, and nineteenth centuries. "Eton Fives" was first played against the school's chapel walls at Eton. The court was similar to the three-wall court used in the United States, except it was much smaller and had some obstacles in the area of play. Another type of handball developed in England, called "Rugby Fives," was played on a four-wall court much like those of the present day. The court was small, measuring only 28' long and 18' wide with walls 15' high, and had no ceiling. Still another game, knows as "Winchester

1

Fives," was played on a court like the Rugby Fives court with a projection called a buttress on the left side of the playing area.

One of the most interesting of the early writings about handball appeared in 1819 in the *London Examiner*. William Hazlitt, obviously a Fives player himself, wrote about the passing of a great player by the name of John Cavanagh:

> When a person dies, who does any one thing better than any one else in the world, which so many others are trying to do well, it leaves a gap in society. Cavanagh is dead and has not left his peer behind him. Whenever he touched the ball there was an end to the chase. His eye was certain, his hand fatal, his presence of mind complete. There was not only nobody equal, but nobody second to him.*

Every country in Ireland had its handball champion, and the game was introduced to the United States in the early 1840s by Irish immigrants. One of the first of these was Phil Casey, who settled in Brooklyn and built the first handball court in America. He has been called the father of handball in the United States. Casey won the first professional world's championship and a $1000 prize.

The lack of adequate spectator space proved to be the downfall of handball as a professional sport. In 1897 the Amateur Athletic Union (A.A.U.) took control of the game and held the first handball tournament in the United States, won by Michael Egan of Jersey City.

The first four-wall handball courts in the United States were much larger than the standard size courts of today. Because of the great expense of construction of four-wall courts, a game played against a single wall, called one-wall handball, developed in the New York area and is still very popular on the East Coast. A three-wall version took hold in the Detroit area, but four-wall handball became the most popular and spread from coast to coast.

The ball first used in the United States, called the hard ball handball, had a cork center with leather strips sewn on the outside, much like the covering of a baseball. Some players used tennis balls with the outer covering removed, but this did not prove satisfactory, and a smaller, faster ball was introduced. This smaller ball, the soft ball handball, soon became more popular than the hard ball, and interest in hard ball matches rapidly dwindled.

---

*Tunis, John R., *Sport for the Fun of it.* (New York, A. S. Barnes and Company, 1940).

Much credit for the development of handball throughout the United States must be given to athletic clubs and Y.M.C.A.s. They built most of the courts and sponsored the first tournaments, and today most courts are found in Y.M.C.A.s and athletic clubs.

Several important dates are significant in the development of handball in the United States:

1915   The first invitational four-wall tournament was held at the Detroit Athletic Club.

1919   The first official A.A.U. National Handball Championships were held in Detroit. Bill Ranft of Los Angeles was the winner.

1924   The first National One-Wall Championships were held in New York; the champion was Jack Byrnes of the West Side "Y."

1925   The first National Y.M.C.A. Championships were held in Cleveland, Ohio, and won by L. A. Walker of Toledo.

1945   The first partial glass court was built at the Town Club in Chicago.

1950   The first National Three-Wall Championships were held in Detroit. The champion was the great Vic Hershkowitz of Brooklyn.

1951   The United States Handball Association (USHA) was formed. Its first national championships were held in Chicago and won by Walter Plekan of Buffalo.

1952   The first National Masters Doubles Championships (one player at least forty years of age and his partner at least forty-five) were held in Detroit. The winners were Bob Kendler and Ray Laser of Chicago.

1953   The first National Intercollegiate Championships, sponsored by the USHA, were held in Chicago.

1956   The first National Juniors Tournament for players under nineteen years of age was held in Chicago and won by Lance Zepp of Buffalo.

1963   A glass amphitheater court with a seating capacity of 1500 persons was constructed at The University of Texas.

1964   The first National Contenders Tournament for players not having won a national championship was held in Milwaukee and won by Dave Graybill of Phoenix.

1966   The first National Masters Singles Championship for players over forty years of age was held in Salt Lake City and won by Vic Hershkowitz of Brooklyn.

The names of the great players and a list of their accomplishments should be included in the history of any sport, and handball has had its share of superstars. Joe Platak of Chicago won the National Four-Wall Championships seven years in succession. Vic Hershkowitz won the National Three-Wall Tournament for nine consecutive years; he also won national championships in four-wall and one-wall handball. Oscar Obert, eldest of the three outstanding handball-playing brothers, won national championships in the four-wall, three-wall, and one-wall games. The greatest of the national four-wall champions was probably Jimmy Jacobs, who started playing in Los Angeles and later moved to New York. Jacobs won more national four-wall championships than any other player in the history of the game.

The player who has done more for the promotion of handball than any other person is Robert Kendler, the first president of the United States Handball Association. Kendler built the first glass handball court which made is possible for handball to develop into a great spectator sport.

Figure 1.1 Action shot of the great Jimmy Jacobs, perhaps the greatest of all the four-wall handball champions.

Handball rewarded him for his contributions to the sport by voting him into the Helms Handball Hall of Fame. Today, handball is an increasingly popular sport. New courts are being constructed all across the United States—at Y.M.C.A.s, athletic clubs, recreation centers, colleges, and universities. There is a quality about the game that seems to invite lifetime addiction. In the early 1800s William Hazlitt remarked of handball:

> The game of fives is what no one despises who has ever played it. It is the finest exercise for the body and the best relaxation for the mind. He who takes to playing at fives is twice young.*

*Ibid.

Terminology

ACE   A perfect service that completely eludes the opponent.

AVOIDABLE HINDER   Illegal interference resulting when a player does not move sufficiently to allow his opponent a shot or when a player lines up so that he will be struck by the ball just played by the opponent.

BACKCOURT   The court area between the short line and the back wall.

BACK WALL SHOT   A shot hit by striking the ball as it rebounds from the back wall.

BOTTOM BOARD KILL   A kill shot hit so low that it does not even bounce on its rebound from the front wall.

CEILING SHOT   A defensive shot that strikes the ceiling before striking the front wall.

CENTER COURT   The area near the short line in the middle of the court that is considered the ideal position of a player when his opponent is hitting the ball.

CHANGEUP   A slow serve executed with a half speed side arm stroke angled so it rebounds toward a rear corner.

CORNER KILL   A kill shot hit toward one of the front corners that strikes two walls before bouncing on the floor.

COURT The area of play. The official size is 20' wide, 20' high, and 40' long, with a back wall at least 12' high.

COURT HINDER An automatic hinder (if the local rules so specify) caused when the ball strikes a court construction obstacle such as a door latch or protruding fan duct.

CROSS CORNER KILL A corner kill shot hit diagonally across court to the front corner opposite the hand that strikes the ball.

CROTCH BALL A ball striking two surfaces at the same time (two walls or a wall and the floor).

CUT OFF The act of hitting the ball as it rebounds from the front wall and before it takes the first bounce on the floor.

CUTTHROAT A game of handball played by three players. It is not an official tournament game.

DEAD BALL Any ball out of play without penalty.

DEFENSIVE SHOT A shot hit to maneuver the opponent into a position close to the back wall.

DIG The retrieving of a low shot before it bounces twice.

DOUBLES The game of handball played by four players, two on each team.

DOUBLES BOX The area in the service zone next to the side walls in which the player must remain until his partner's serve has crossed the short line.

DRIVE The act of hitting the ball against the front wall with enough power so that it rebounds fast.

ENGLISH The spin applied when striking the ball in order to make it *"hook."*

ERROR The failure to make a legal return when the player's hand has hit the ball.

FAULT An illegally served ball that involves a penalty.

FIST BALL A ball struck with a closed fist.

FLAT KILL See *"Bottom Board Kill."*

FLY BALL See *"Cut Off."*

FOOT FAULT A fault by the server that occurs when one or both feet are outside the service zone at some time during the execution of the serve.

FOUR-WALL HANDBALL The most popular form of handball that is played inside an enclosed four walled court.

FREEZE OUT The particular strategy in doubles in which both players on a team attempt to direct all of their shots toward one of the players on the opposing team, thereby "freezing out" his partner.

FRONT COURT   The court area between the short line and the front wall.

GAME   The unit completed by one player or team scoring 21 points first.

HANDOUT   The loss of service by the player on a doubles team who is the first server on that team.

HINDER   Accidental interference with an opponent, or obstruction of the flight of the ball not involving penalty.

HIT   The act of striking the ball when attempting a shot.

HOOK   A ball that breaks to the left or right after rebounding from the front wall and striking the floor.

HOP   See *"Hook."*

INNING   The time in which a player or team holds the service.

INSIDE CORNER KILL   A corner kill shot in which the ball strikes the front wall first.

IRISH WHIP   The arm stroke in which the ball is contacted close to the body with an underarm motion.

KILL   A scoring shot hit so low against the front wall that the opponent cannot make a legal return.

LEFT SIDE PLAYER   The partner in doubles having responsibility for coverage of the left side of the court.

LOB   A serve or shot hit high and easy against the front wall so that it drops steeply and takes a high bounce to the rear of the court.

LONG   A served ball that first hits the front wall and rebounds to the back wall before touching the floor. It is also called a *"short"* service.

MATCH   The best two out of three games.

NATURAL HOOK   A ball that breaks to the left (if hit with the right hand) after rebounding from the front wall and striking the floor. (The break is to the right if the ball is struck by the left hand.)

OFFENSIVE POSITION   The position a player assumes when he has time to set his feet before striking the ball and when he can hit his shot with a sidearm or underarm stroke.

ONE-WALL HANDBALL   A form of handball played on a court having only one wall. This court does not have side walls, a back wall, or a ceiling.

OUT   Loss of service by a singles player or by both players on a doubles team.

OUTSIDE CORNER KILL   A corner kill shot in which the ball strikes the side wall before hitting the front wall.

OVERHAND STROKE   The arm stroke used when hitting the ball from a shoulder high or higher position. Most defensive shots are hit with an overhand stroke.

PASS SHOT   A scoring shot hit at such an angle that it rebounds out of the opponent's reach on either side.

POINT   A tally scored by the serving side.

RALLY   The period of play after the ball is served until one side fails to make a legal return.

RECEIVER   The player or players to whom the ball is served.

REFEREE   The official of a tournament match who decides all questions that may arise during the match.

REVERSE HOOK   A ball that breaks to the right (if hit with the right hand) after rebounding from the front wall and striking the floor. (The break is to the left if the ball is struck with the left hand.)

RIGHT SIDE PLAYER   The partner in doubles having responsibility for coverage of the right side of the court.

ROLLOUT   See *"Bottom Board Kill."*

SCORER   An official in a tournament match who keeps a record of the order of the service, the outs, and the points made.

SCOTCH TWIST   A serve angled so that it will strike the front wall very close to a corner. It then strikes the side wall and rebounds diagonally toward the opposite side wall near the back wall.

SEMIGLASS COURT   A handball court in which a part of the side wall(s) and/or back wall is constructed of glass instead of the usual concrete and plaster.

SERVE   The act of putting the ball into play.

SERVER   The player serving the ball.

SERVICE LINE   The line parallel to and 15' from the front wall.

SERVICE ZONE   The court area between the service and short line from which the server is required to serve the ball.

SETUP   A ball in play that gives a player an easy opportunity to execute a scoring shot.

SHADOW SERVE   An illegally served ball not involving penalty that passes so close to the server that the receiver does not see the ball until it is too late to make the return.

SHOOT   The act of attempting a kill shot.

SHORT   An illegal serve which involves a "fault" or penalty on the server.

SHORT LINE   The line running parallel with the front wall and dividing the court into two equal divisions.

SIDE ARM STROKE   The arm stroke used in hitting a shot when the ball is at a waist high or lower position. The fingers point toward the side wall when contacting the ball.

SIDE OUT   See *"Out."*

SINGLES   The game of handball played by two players.

SKIP IN   An attempted return that is illegal because the ball strikes the floor just before making contact with the front wall.

THREE-WALL HANDBALL   A form of handball played on a court having a front wall and two side walls but no back wall or ceiling.

THREE-WALL JAI-ALAI COURT   A court having a front wall, one side wall, and a back wall.

THREE-WALL RETURN   A defensive shot that strikes three walls (sidewall, front wall, sidewall) before hitting the floor.

TRAP SHOT   A ball struck very close to the floor and immediately after it bounces on the floor.

UNDERARM STROKE   The arm motion in which the ball is contacted below the waist line with the fingers pointing toward the floor.

UNIFORM   The playing attire. In official tournament competition the player is required to wear a white uniform consisting of shirt, pants, shoes, and socks.

VOLLEY   See *"Cut Off."*

WEAK ARM   The nondominant arm of a player.

Z-SERVE   See *"Scotch Twist."*

Rules

The following are the official rules for four-wall handball published by the United States Handball Association. The rules for one-wall handball and three-wall handball are basically the same as those for four-wall handball. There are a few exceptions, however, and these are mentioned at the end of the chapter.

OFFICIAL U.S. HANDBALL ASSOCIATION FOUR-WALL HANDBALL RULES

Part I. The Game

Rule 1.1-Types of Games. Four-wall handball may be played by two or four players. When played by two it is called "singles"; and when played by four, "doubles."

Rule 1.2-Description. Handball, as the name implies, is a competitive game in which either hand or fist may be used to serve and return the ball.

Rule 1.3-Objective. The objective is to win each volley by serving or returning the ball so the opponent is unable to keep the ball in play. A serve or volley is won when a side is unable to return the ball before it touches the floor twice.

Rule 1.4-Points and Outs. Points are scored only by the serving side when it serves an ace or wins

Figure 3.1 Four-wall handball court at The University of Texas at Austin: Note that the back and side walls are constructed of glass allowing for a spectator capacity of 1200 persons.

a volley. When the serving side loses a volley it loses the serve which is called an "out" in singles, and a "hand-out" in doubles.

Rule 1.5-Game. A game is won by the side first scoring 21 points.

Rule 1.6-Match. A match is won by the side first winning two games.

Part II. Court and Equipment

Rule 2.1-Court. The specifications for the standard four-wall handball court are:

a. Dimensions. The dimensions shall be 20' wide, 20' high, and 40' long, with back wall at least 12' high.

b. Lines and Zones. Handball courts shall be divided and marked on the floors with 1½" wide red or white lines as follows:

1. **Short Line.** The short line is midway between and is parallel with the front and back walls dividing the court into equal front and back courts.

2. **Service Line.** The service line is parallel with and located 5' in front of the short line

3. **Service Zone.** The service zone is the space between the outer edges of the short and service lines.

4. **Service Boxes.** A service box is located at each end of the service zone by lines 18" from and parallel with each side wall.

5. **Receiving Lines.** Five feet back of the short line, vertical lines shall be marked on each side wall extending 3" from the floor. See rule 4.7(a).

Figure 3.2 Standard official dimensions of the four-wall handball court.

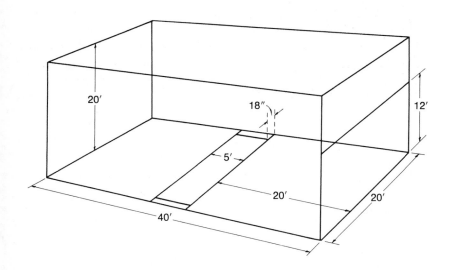

Rule 2.2-Ball Specifications. The specifications for the standard handball are:

Material: Rubber

Color: Black

Size: 1 7/8" diameter, with 1/32" variation.

Weight: (2.3) oz., with a variation of 2/10 oz.

Rebound from 70" drop—42 to 48" at a temperature of 68°.

Rule 2.3-Ball Selection. A new ball shall be selected by the referee for use in each match in all tournaments. During a game the referee may, at his discretion or at the request of both players or teams, select another ball. Balls that are not round or which bounce erratically shall not be used. The Spalding ACE handball is official for all U.S. Handball Association sanctioned tournaments.

Rule 2.4-Gloves. Handball may not be played barehanded. Gloves must be worn. Gloves shall be light in color and made of a soft material or leather, and form fitting. The fingers of the gloves may not be webbed or connected, nor removed. No foreign substance, tape or rubber bands shall be used on the fingers or on the palms of the gloves. No metal or hard substance may be worn on the hand under the glove. For sensitive, bruised or sore hands etc., surgical gauze or tape may be wrapped around palm of hand with or without thin foam rubber for protective purposes. The gloves must be changed when they become sufficiently wet to moisten the ball. Players should have an ample supply of dry gloves for each match.

Rule 2.5-Uniform. All parts of the uniform, consisting of a shirt, shorts, socks and shoes, shall be clean and white. Warmup shirts and pants, if worn in actual match play, shall also be white. Only club insignia and/or name of club or handball organization may be on the uniform. Players may not play without shirts.

Part III. Officiating

Rule 3.1-Tournaments. All tournaments shall be managed by a committee or chairman, who shall designate the officials.

Rule 3.2-Officials. The officials shall include a referee and a scorer. Additional assistants and record keepers may be designated as desired.

Rule 3.3-Qualifications. Since the quality of the officiating often determines the success of each tournament, all officials shall be experienced or trained, and shall be thoroughly familiar with these rules and with the local playing conditions.

Rule 3.4-Rule Briefing. Before all tournaments, all officials and players shall be briefed on rules and on local court hinders or other regulations.

Rule 3.5-Referees.

a. Pre-Match Duties. Before each match commences, it shall be the duty of the referee to:

1. Check on adequacy of preparation of the handball court with respect to cleanliness, lighting and temperature, and upon location of locker rooms, drinking fountains, etc.
2. Check on availability and suitability of all materials necessary for the match such as handballs, towels, score cards and pencils.
3. Check readiness and qualifications of assisting officials.
4. Explain court regulations to players and inspect the compliance of gloves and hands with rules.
5. Remind players to have an adequate supply of extra gloves and shirts.
6. Introduce players, toss coin, and signal start of first game.

b. Decisions. During games the referee shall decide all questions that may arise in accordance with these rules. If there is body contact on the back swing, the player should call it quickly. This is the only call a player may make. See Rule 4.10(b). On all questions involving judgment and on all questions not covered by these rules, the decision of the referee is final.

c. Protests. Any decision not involving the judgment of the referee may on protest be decided by the chairman, if present, or his delegated representative.

d. Forfeitures. A match may be forfeited by the referee when:

1. Any player refuses to abide by the referee's decision or engages in unsportsmanlike conduct.
2. After warning any player leaves the court without permission of the referee either during a game or between the first and second games.
3. Any player for a singles match, or any team for a doubles match fails to report to play. Normally, 20 minutes from the scheduled

game time will be allowed before forfeiture. The tournament chairman may permit a longer delay if circumstances warrant such a decision.

4. If both players for a singles, or both teams for doubles fail to appear to play for consolation matches or other playoffs, they shall forfeit their ratings for future tournaments, and forfeit any trophies, medals, or awards. See Rule 5.4.

Rule 3.6-Scorers. The scorer shall keep a record of the progress of the game in the manner prescribed by the committee or chairman. As a minimum the progress record shall include the order of serves, outs, and points. The referee or scorer shall announce the score before each serve.

Rule 3.7-Record Keepers. In addition to the scorer, the committee may designate additional persons to keep more detailed records for statistical purposes of the progress of the game.

Part IV. Play Regulations

Rule 4.1-Serve-Generally.

a. Order. The player or side winning the toss becomes the first server and starts the first game, and the third game, if any.

b. Start. Games are started by the referee calling "play ball."

c. Place. The server may serve from any place in the service zone. No part of either foot may extend beyond either line of the service zone. Stepping on the line (but not beyond it) is permitted. Server must remain in the service zone until the served ball passes short line. Violations are called "foot faults." See Rule 4.5(a)(1).

d. Manner. A serve is commenced by bouncing the ball to the floor in the service zone, and on the first bounce the ball is struck by the server's hand or fist so that it hits the front wall and on the rebound hits the floor back of the short line, either with or without touching one of the side walls.

e. Readiness. Serves shall not be made until the receiving side is ready, or the referee has called play ball.

Rule 4.2-Serve-In Doubles.

a. Server. At the beginning of each game in doubles, each side shall inform the referee of the order of service, which order shall be followed throughout the game. Only the first server serves the first time up and continues to serve first throughout the game. When the first server is out, the side is out. Thereafter both players on each side shall serve until a hand-out occurs. It is not necessary for the server to alternate serves to their opponents.

b. Partner's Position. On each serve, the server's partner shall stand erect with his back to the side wall and with both feet on the floor within the service box until the served ball passes the short line. Violations are called "foot faults." See Rule 4.5 (a)(2).

Rule 4.3-Defective Serves. Defective serves are of three types resulting in penalties as follows:

a. Dead Ball Serve. A dead ball serve results in no penalty and the server is given another serve without cancelling a prior illegal serve. For details see Rule 4.4.

b. Fault Serve. Two fault serves results in a hand-out. For details see Rule 4.5.

c. Out Serves. An out serve results in a hand-out. For details see Rule 4.6.

Rule 4.4-Dead Ball Serves. Dead ball serves do not cancel any previous illegal serve. They occur when an otherwise legal serve:

a. Hits Partner. Hits the server's partner on the fly on the rebound from the front wall while the server's partner is in the service box. Any serve that touches the floor before hitting the partner in the box is a short. See Rule 4.6 (c).

b. Screen Balls. Passes too close to the server or the server's partner to obstruct the view of the returning side. Any serve passing behind the server's partner and the side wall is an automatic screen. See Rule 4.10(a)(4).

c. Court Hinders. Hits any part of the court that under local rules is a dead ball. See Rule 4.10(a)(1).

Rule 4.5-Fault Serves. The following serves are faults and any two in succession results in a handout:

a. Foot Faults. A foot fault results:

1. When the server leaves the service zone before the served ball passes the short line. See Rule 4.1(c).
2. When the server's partner leaves the service box before the served ball passes the short line. See Rule 4.1(c).

b. Short Serve. A short serve is any served ball that first hits the front wall and on the rebound hits the floor in front of the back edge of the short line either with or without touching one side wall; or

c. Two-Side Serve. A two-side serve is any ball served that first hits the front wall and on the rebound hits two side walls on the fly.

d. Ceiling Serve. A ceiling serve is any served ball that touches the ceiling after hitting the front wall either with or without touching one side wall.

e. Long Serve. A long serve is any served ball that first hits the front wall and rebounds to the back wall before touching the floor.

f. Out of Court Serve. Any ball going out of the court on the serve. See also Rule 4.9(f).

g. Crotch Serve. If the served ball hits the crotch in the front wall it is considered the same as hitting the floor and is an out. To be consistent a crotch serve into the back wall is good and in play.

Rule 4.6-Out Serves. Any one of the following serves results in a hand-out:

a. Bounces. Bouncing the ball more than three times while in the service zone before striking the ball. A bounce is a drop or throw to the floor, followed by a catch. The ball may not be bounced anywhere but on the floor within the service zone. Accidental dropping of the ball counts as one bounce.

b. Missed Ball. Any attempt to strike the ball on the first bounce that results either in a total miss or in touching any part of the server's body other than his serving hand or fist.

c. Non-front Serve. Any served ball that strikes the server's partner, or the ceiling, floor or side wall, before striking the front wall.

d. Touched Serve. Any served ball that on the rebound from the front wall touches the server, or touches the server's partner while any part of his body is out of the service box—(See Rule 4.4(a)—or the server's partner intentionally catches the served ball on the fly.

e. Out-of-Order Serve. In doubles, when either partner serves out of order, or serves both hands.

Rule 4.7-Return of Serve.

a. Receiving Position. The receiver or receivers must stand at least 5′ back of the short line, as indicated by the 3″ vertical line on each side wall, until the ball is struck by the server. See Rule 2.1(b)(5). After a warning, any infraction of this rule by a receiver results in a point for the server.

b. Defective Serve. To eliminate any misunderstanding, the receiving side should not catch or touch a defectively served ball until called by the referee or it has touched the floor the second time.

c. Fly Return. In making a fly return the receiver must end up with both feet back of the service zone. A violation by a receiver results in a point for the server.

d. Legal Return. After the ball is legally served, one of the players on the receiving side must strike the ball either on the fly or after the first bounce and before the ball touches the floor the second time to return the ball to the front wall either directly or after touching one or both side walls, the back wall or the ceiling, or any combination of those surfaces. A returned ball may not touch the floor before touching the front wall.

e. Failure to Return. The failure to return a serve results in a point for the server.

f. Touching Receiver. See Rule 4.9(e).

Rule 4.8-Changes of Serve.

a. Hand-out. A server is entitled to continue serving until:

1. **Out Serve.** He makes an out serve under Rule 4.6, or
2. **Fault Serves.** He makes two fault serves in succession under Rule 4.5, or
3. **Hits Partner.** He hits his partner with an attempted return before the ball touches the floor the second time.
4. **Return Failure.** He or his partner fails to keep the ball in play by returning it as required by Rule 4.7(d).
5. **Avoidable Hinder.** He or his partner commits an avoidable hinder under Rule 4.11.

b. Side-out.

1. **In Singles.** In singles, retiring the server retires the side.
2. **In Doubles.** In doubles, the side is retired when both partners have been put out, except on the first serve as provided in Rule 4.2(a).

c. Effect. When the server or the side loses the serve, the server or serving side shall become the receiver; and the receiving side, the server; and so alternately in all subsequent services of the game.

Rule 4.9-Volleys. Each legal return after the serve is called a volley. Play during volleys shall be according to the following rules:

a. One Hand. Only front or back of one hand or fist may be used at any one time to return the ball. Using two hands to hit a ball is out. The use of the foot or any portion of the body, other than the hand or fist is an out.

b. Wrist Ball. The use of any other part of the body including the wrist or arm above the player's hand to return the ball is prohibited.

c. One Touch. In attempting returns, the ball may be touched only once by one player on returning side. In doubles both partners may swing at, but only one, may hit the ball. Each violation of (a), (b), or (c) results in a hand-out or point.

d. Return Attempts.

1. **In Singles.** In singles if a player swings at but misses the ball in play, the player may repeat his attempts to return the ball until it touches the floor the second time.

2. **In Doubles.** In doubles if one player swings at but misses the ball, both he and his partner may make further attempts to return the ball until it touches the floor the second time. Both partners on a side are entitled to an attempt to return the ball.

3. **Hinders.** In singles or doubles, if a player swings at but misses the ball in play, and in his, or his partner's attempt again to play the ball there is an unintentional interference by an opponent it shall be a hinder. See Rule 4.10.

e. Touching Ball. Except as provided in Rule 4.10(a)(2), any touching of a ball before it touches the floor the second time by a player other than the one making a return is a point or out against the offending player.

f. Out of Court Ball.

1. **After Return.** Any ball returned to the front wall which on the rebound or on the first bounce goes into the gallery or through any opening in a side wall shall be declared dead and the serve replayed.

2. **No Return.** Any ball not returned to the front wall, but which caroms off a player's hand or fist into the gallery or into any opening in a side wall either with or without touching the ceiling,

side or back wall, shall be an out or point against the player failing to make the return. See also Rule 4.5(f).

g. Dry Ball and Gloves. During the game and particularly on service every effort should be made to keep the ball dry. Deliberately wetting shall result in an out. The ball may be inspected by the referee at any time during a game. If a player's gloves are wet to the extent that they leave wet marks on the ball, the player shall change to dry gloves on a referee's time out. If a player wishes to change to dry gloves, he shall hold the palms up to the referee and get the referee's permission to change. He may not leave the court without the referee's permission.

h. Broken Ball. If there is any suspicion that a ball has broken on the serve or during a volley, play shall continue until the end of the volley. The referee or any player may request the ball be examined. If the referee decides the ball is broken or otherwise defective, a new ball shall be put into play and the point replayed.

i. Play Stoppage. If a player loses a shoe or other equipment, or foreign objects enter the court, or any other outside interference occurs, the referee shall stop the play.

Rule 4.10-Dead Ball Hinders. Hinders are of two types—"dead ball" and "avoidable." Dead ball hinders as described in this rule results in the point being replayed. Avoidable hinders are described in Rule 4.11.

a. Situations. -When called by the referee, the following are dead ball hinders:

1. **Court Hinders.** Hits any part of the court which under local rules is a dead ball.

2. **Hitting Opponent.** Any returned ball that touches an opponent on the fly before it returns to the front wall.

3. **Body Contact.** Any body contact with an opponent that interferes with seeing or returning the ball.

4. **Screen Ball.** Any ball rebounding from the front wall close to the body of a player on the side which just returned the ball, to interfere with or prevent the returning side from seeing the ball. See Rule 4.4(b).

5. **Straddle Ball.** A ball passing between the legs of a player on the side which just returned the ball, if there is no fair chance to see or return the ball.

6. Other Interference. Any other unintentional interference which prevents an opponent from having a fair chance to see or return the ball.

b. Effect. A call by the referee of a "hinder" stops the play and voids any situation following, such as the ball hitting a player. No player is authorized to call a hinder, except on the back swing and such a call must be made immediately as provided in Rule 3.5(b).

c. Avoidance. While making an attempt to return the ball, a player is entitled to a fair chance to see and return the ball. It is the duty of the side that has just served or returned the ball to move so that the receiving side may go straight to the ball and not be required to go around an opponent. The referee should be liberal in calling hinders to discourage any practice of playing the ball where an adversary cannot see it until too late. It is no excuse that the ball is "killed," unless in the opinion of the referee he couldn't return the ball. Hinders should be called without a claim by a player, especially in close plays and on game points. It is not a hinder when one player hinders his partner.

d. In Doubles. In doubles, both players on a side are entitled to a fair and unobstructed chance at the ball and either one is entitled to a hinder even though it naturally would be his partner's ball and even though his partner may have attempted to play the ball or that he may already have missed it.

Rule 4.11-Avoidable Hinders. An avoidable hinder results in an "out" or a "point" depending upon whether the offender was serving or receiving.

a. Failure to Move. Does not move sufficiently to allow opponent his shot.

b. Blocking. Moves into a position effecting a block, on the opponent about to return the ball, or, in doubles, one partner moves in front of an opponent as his partner is returning the ball, or

c. Moving into Ball. Moves in the way and is struck by the ball just played by his opponent.

d. Pushing. Deliberately pushing or shoving an opponent during a volley.

Rule 4.12-Rest Periods.

a. Delays. Deliberate delay exceeding ten seconds by server, or receiver shall result in an out or point against the offender.

b. During Game. During a game each player in singles, or each side in doubles, either while serving or receiving may request a "time out" for a towel, wiping glasses, change or adjust equipment. Each "time out" shall not exceed 30 seconds. No more than three "time outs" in a game shall be granted each singles player or to each team in doubles.

c. Injury. No time out shall be charged to a player who is injured during play. An injured player shall not be allowed more than a total of 15 minutes of rest. If the injured player is not able to resume play after total rests of 15 minutes the match shall be awarded to the opponent or opponents. On any further injury to same player, the Commissioner, if present, or committee, after considering any available medical opinion shall determine whether the injured player will be allowed to continue.

d. Between Games. A 2 minute rest period is allowed between the first and second games, at which times the players should NOT leave the court, without approval of the referee. A 10 minute rest period is allowed between the second and third games, at which time players may leave the court.

e. Postponed Games. Any games postponed by referee due to weather elements shall be resumed with the same score as when postponed.

Part V. Tournaments

Rule 5.1-Draws. If possible, the singles draw shall be made at least two days before the tournament commences. The seeding method of drawing shall be approved by the committee or chairman.

Rule 5.2-Scheduling

a. Preliminary Matches. If one or more contestants are entered in both singles and doubles, they may be required to play both singles and doubles on the same day or night with little rest between matches. This is a risk assumed on entering both singles and doubles. If possible the schedule should provide at least a one hour rest period between all matches.

b. Final Matches. Where one or more players have reached the finals in both singles and doubles, it is recommended that the doubles match be played on the day preceding the singles. This would assure more rest between the final matches. If both final matches must be played on the same day or night, the following procedure is recommended:

1. The singles match be played first.
2. A rest period of not less than ONE HOUR be allowed between the finals in singles and doubles.

Rule 5.3-Notice of Matches. After the first round of matches, it is the responsibility of each player to check the posted schedules to determine the time and place of each subsequent match. If any change is made in the schedule after posting, it shall be the duty of the committee or chairman to notify the players of the change.

ONE-WALL AND THREE-WALL RULES

Basically handball rules for one-wall, three-wall and four-wall are the same with the following exceptions:

One-Wall

COURT SIZE   Wall shall be 20′ in width and 16′ high, floor 20′ in width and 34′ from the wall to the back edge of the long line. There should be a minimum of 3′ beyond the long line and 6′ outside each side line. There should be minimum of 6′ outside each side line and behind the long line to permit movement area for the players.

SHORT   LINE   Back   edge   16′   from   the   wall.   SERVICE MARKERS   Lines at least 6″ long parallel to and midway between the long and short lines, extending in from the side lines. The imaginary extension and joining of these lines indicates the SERVICE LINE. LINES are 1½″ in width. SERVICE ZONE floor area inside and including the short, side and service lines. RECEIVING ZONE floor area in back of short line bounded by and including the long and side lines.

REFEREEING   In one-wall an additional duty is that of linesman for each sideline . . . duties to call out the balls that hit the floor or the wall off the court and to call any faults.

LEGAL BLOCK   Big difference in one-wall is "Standing Still In Front Or Aside" allowed. If a player attempting to play a ball is interfered with by an opponent, who, after his side had played the ball, was perfectly still in front or aside the player it is NOT a hinder. This "legal block" is the essence of the one-wall game. However, if a player of the side that has just hit the ball stands perfectly still, but the opponent moves back into him in trying to play the ball, and is thus kept from having a chance to

Figure 3.3 One-wall handball court at the Brownsville Boy's Club, Brooklyn, N. Y. Howie Eisenberg makes a diving return of a ball hit by Steve Sandler at the National One-Wall Championships.

Photograph taken by Egon Teichert and shown here courtesy of the United States Handball Association.

play the ball, it is a hinder. It is the duty of the man in back to get out of the way.

Three-Wall

SERVE   A serve that goes beyond the side walls on the fly is player or side out. A serve that goes beyond the long line on a fly but within the side walls is the same as a "short."

Figure 3.4   Three-wall handball court at Palmer Park, Detroit, Michigan. Oscar Obert makes the long return against opponents Paul Haber and Dennis Hofflander, in the front court, while Ruby Obert looks on at the National Three-Wall Championships.

Picture taken by Egon Teichert and shown here through the courtesy of the United States Handball Association.

Fundamentals

Uniform and Equipment

The proper dress for playing handball is an all-white uniform including white gym shorts, a T-shirt, socks, and tennis shoes. You will also need a pair of handball gloves and a handball. Several different styles of gloves are available at most sporting goods stores. Try the gloves on to be sure of a comfortable fit. Don't buy gloves that are so tight fitting they restrict the bending of the fingers. It is better to have gloves slightly large than too small.

Hand Position and Ball Contact

When hitting the handball, hold your hand in a relaxed cup, as illustrated in Figure 4.1. Hold your fingers together with the thumb lined up beside the first finger. Make certain not to tense your fingers so tight that your wrist will not flex. Your wrist should be loose and flexible for most shots.

Contact the ball at the base of the first two fingers, as illustrated in Figure 4.2. This is where you would grip the ball if you were going to throw it like a baseball. Although you can strike the ball further down in the palm area, you will have better control and leverage if you hit it at the base of the fingers.

Figure 4.1   Hand position when striking ball.

Figure 4.2   Contact is made at base of the first two fingers.

THE STROKES

On all strokes you should face the right side wall if you are going to hit a right-handed shot or the left side wall if you are attempting a left-handed shot. The same fundamentals apply as when throwing a baseball. Face the side wall and spread your feet approximately 12″. Flex your knees slightly and rest your weight on the balls of your feet even though your entire foot is on the floor.

Most of your weight is on your back foot (the right foot if you are facing the right wall; the left foot if you are facing the left wall) at the start of the stroke and is shifted to your front foot as you stride toward the front wall to begin your stroke. All of your weight is on your front foot at the end of the stroke.

In preparing to stroke the ball, with your weight on your back foot, cock your shoulders and hips as you draw your arm back in a backswing position. As you bring your arm forward into the stroke, rotate your shoulders and hips toward the front wall, utilizing your full body weight for the hit. If you used only arm motion to make the shot, your arm would soon tire and become ineffective.

The arm stroke used in hitting a handball is the same as the arm motion used in throwing a baseball. Beginners often make the mistake of tightening their arm and wrist, which causes them to stroke the ball like a tennis ball. You must keep your arm and wrist relaxed in order to get a smooth throwing swing with a good follow through on your arm stroke. Draw your arm back as far as it will go. You can bend your elbow either slightly or even as much as 90°, depending on which feels more natural. As you step into the ball, move your arm forward, with the elbow leading, and break your relaxed, cocked wrist as contact is made with the ball. Your forearm should snap forward after contact, and your arm should continue smoothly in a full follow-through motion. You might almost say that the ball is whipped or flung to the front wall.

The ideal point of contact is on a line with the middle of the body. The ball should be far enough away from the body to allow the arm to be almost fully extended as contact is made.

There are four basic armstrokes: (1) the *Overhand Stroke*; (2) the *Sidearm Stroke*; (3) the *Low Sidearm Stroke*; and (4) the *Underhand Stroke*.

The Overhand Stroke

The overhand stroke is usually the most natural stroke for the beginning player. This is the stroke used to return high bounding balls from a shoulder high or higher position, and to hit ceiling shots and lob serves as described in Chapters 5 and 6. Notice in Figure 4.3 that the elbow is pointing downward and the fingers are pointing toward the ceiling at the point of contact. Figure 4.4 shows the point of contact of ball and hand for the overhand stroke.

The Sidearm Stroke

The sidearm stroke is used to hit returns between the thigh and the chest and to execute the pass shot discussed in Chapter 6. Figure 4.5 illustrates how the elbow is drawn straight back in preparation. Notice in Figure 4.6 that the point of contact is on a line with the center of the body and away from the body so that the arm is almost fully extended and the forearm and fingers point toward the sidewall. You should crouch slightly when attempting this stroke.

Figure 4.3 The overhand stroke.

Figure 4.4   Point of contact for the overhand stroke.

The Low Sidearm Stroke

The low sidearm stroke is identical to the sidearm stroke just discussed, except that contact with the ball is made much closer to the floor. The knees and waist must be bent more in order to assume a lower crouched position. Whenever possible, you should attempt your shot from this position. The low sidearm stroke is perhaps the most important of all the handball strokes. It is used most often in executing the kill shots described in Chapter 6. Again (see Fig. 4.7), the forearm should be parallel to the floor and the fingers pointing toward the side wall when contact is made, although some players hit the ball with the forearm pointing slightly downward.

The Underhand Stroke

As Figure 4.8 illustrates, for the underhand stroke the ball is close to the body and the forearm and fingers point toward the floor when contact is made. The arm is raised to about shoulder level on the backswing, and the forward downward swing is like that of a softball pitcher. The underarm stroke is often used in executing the advanced fist ceiling shot discussed in Chapter 6. When the handball courts were much larger than

Figure 4.5   The sidearm stroke.

Figure 4.6 Point of contact for the sidearm stroke.

present regulation size, the underhand stroke was considered the most important stroke in the game. But greater accuracy is required on the smaller court, and players have found that the low sidearm stroke is more accurate for low kill shots. Except for the fist ceiling shot, most good players use the underhand stroke only when the ball is very close to the body and they do not have time or room to move away from the ball before attempting their shot.

FOOTWORK

Since the ball rarely comes to you in perfect position to be hit, you must move into the proper position. Footwork is one of the most important fundamentals of handball. Good footwork begins with an alert starting position, as illustrated in Figure 4.9. The body is slightly crouched, with the knees flexed and the weight on the balls of the feet. The forearms are drawn up so that they are parallel with the floor.

As soon as you see the direction of the ball, move quickly to the court position from which you will attempt your shot. Remember, you should face a side wall when attempting a shot, so don't move directly

Figure 4.7 The low sidearm stroke: Note the height of ball as contact is made, and player's follow-through position.

Figure 4.8 The underhand stroke.

behind the ball but rather to one side or the other of it, depending on which hand you will use for the shot attempt. Always finish your move into position in such a manner that the weight of your body is traveling

Figure 4.9 "Ready position" when opponent is about to contact his shot.

into the shot and toward the front wall. Prepare for your stroke as you are moving for your shot by drawing your arm back partially (see Fig. 4.10), and complete the backswing as you set your feet for the shot.

Whether you are moving forward, backward, or sideways, keep your eyes on the ball at all times.

WHEN TO STROKE THE BALL

Beginners often make the mistake of rushing shots and trying to hit the ball too soon. The best time to hit the ball is after it has reached the height of its bounce and is dropping toward the floor. It is very difficult to hit the ball as it is bouncing up from the floor, and good players seldom attempt this. Figure 4.11 illustrates the best places to hit the shot. Position number one is the best place for the beginner to attempt his return. A hit in position number two is a fly or volley shot—an important shot that requires greater timing because there is less time in which to get into good position. A hit in position number three is a trap shot, hitting the ball just

Figure 4.10 Player moving to position for shot attempt: Note arm moving to position.

after it contacts the floor. The underhand stroke is used to hit the ball in this position.

PROGRAM OF PROGRESSION

Following is a day-by-day progression program for the beginning player.

First Day. Your first efforts should be directed toward getting the feel of the handball and of being inside the handball court. Begin by standing a few feet behind the short line and throwing the ball to the front wall, using the various arm strokes described previously. Throw first with your strong arm, being sure to face the side wall and to stride forward as you release the ball. Try to aim at a certain spot on the front wall and catch the ball on the first bounce. Turn around and duplicate the throw with your weak arm.

Handball is unique in that it requires the efficient use of both hands, and thus *one of your major objectives should be to develop your* **weak**

Figure 4.11 Three places to contact ball. (1) For beginners. (2) A "fly shot." (3) A "trap shot."

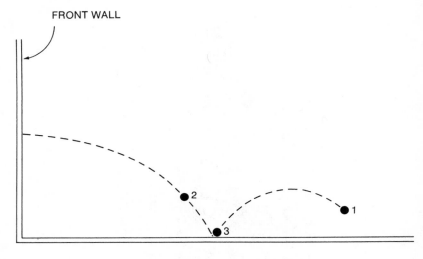

FRONT WALL

arm. Weak arm skills are not easily learned, so begin the very first day by concentrating much of your efforts on this. Since you hit a handball with the same arm motion that you use to throw a baseball, throwing a handball with your weak arm is good practice. This will help develop skill and coordination to improve the hitting action. Don't try to aim your weak hand throws. Face the side wall and stride toward the front wall as you whip your arm forward.

A good throwing motion is a highly coordinated muscular act, and the most important part of the action is proper feet and body position. Often the beginner does something obviously wrong with his weak arm, but since he can't see himself, he continues to make the same mistakes. One of the best ways to avoid this is to stand in front of a full-length mirror and first throw with your strong arm, noticing all the details of the action, including body position, the back swing of the arm, the way the wrist is held, the manner in which the elbow leads the throw, the follow through, and the way the shoulders and hips are cocked on the backswing and rotate on the throw. Notice also what the arm that isn't throwing does—such as the way it comes back on the backswing and the way it leads the shoulder rotation into the shot. Next turn around and try to duplicate the throwing motion with your weak arm, putting together all of the details involved in the smooth throwing motion. The weak arm development will be a slow process, but there will be progress if you work hard to overcome this weakness.

Spend your first day in the court just throwing the ball. Throw the ball at different angles, heights, and speeds, watching and learning how it reacts on the rebound. Always attempt to move into a position so you can catch the ball on the first bounce. You must learn the court angles in order to be in proper position for your shot attempt.

Don't throw the ball as hard as you can. There is no reason ever to do this, and the only thing you might get out of it is a sore arm. Begin by throwing half-speed, and gradually begin to throw harder, but never as hard as you can.

Throw the ball with all the different arm strokes, but spend most of the time throwing with the sidearm and low sidearm strokes. Throw the ball as often with your weak hand as with your strong hand.

Second Day. Spend the first 10 or 15 minutes throwing the ball as you did the first day. Continue to concentrate your efforts on your weak arm. Try to catch all of your tosses on the first bounce, and try to face a side wall as you make your catch so that you will be in position to hit your return. Try to catch the ball in the center of and away from your body in this position.

Spend the remainder of the period dropping the ball to the floor, and on its rebound step into the ball and stroke it to the front wall. Remember, try to contact the ball at the base of the fingers. Attempt your hitting stroke with the identical arm and body motion used when throwing the ball. Start by facing a side wall and holding the ball in the opposite hand from the one you are going to use for the stroke. Drop the ball to the floor from about waist high, and be sure it is far enough away from your body so you can reach it with your natural throwing stroke. Draw your arm back as if you were getting ready to throw the ball. Wait for the ball to reach the height of its bounce and step toward the front wall, making contact with the ball as it starts to drop. Don't forget the good follow through arm motion after contact. Next, turn around and duplicate the shot with your weak arm. Don't overswing by hitting the ball too hard. Rather, try to stroke the ball with a three-quarter speed arm stroke.

It is important to warm up your hands before beginning, or you may find that they sting when you strike the ball. This can result in a bone bruise, unless you take preliminary precautions. You can warm up your hands by clapping them together several times or by placing them in a basin of hot water and keeping them there for several minutes before playing. Many top handball players do this before playing, regardless of the temperature of the courts.

Third Day. Spend the first 10 minutes throwing the ball. Keep working on your weak arm. Throw the ball at all angles and catch the ball on the first bounce, facing a side wall. Next, drop the ball to the floor and stroke the ball to the front wall as you did the second day. Spend about 10 minutes on this drill.

Spend the remainder of the period tossing the ball to the front wall, moving into position, and hitting the ball back to the front wall. Begin by standing in the service zone and tossing the ball with an easy underhand stroke to the front wall, allowing yourself time to move into the proper position and get set before attempting the shot. Review the sections on *Footwork* and *When to Stroke the Ball.* Remember to move to the side of the ball. Contact the ball with your arm on a line with the middle of your body, and be sure the ball is not so close to you that your swing is cramped. Toss the ball at all angles, and attempt the various strokes with both arms. Gradually move deeper in the court, and remember that the arm stroke should be a throwing motion with the arm and wrist loose so the ball can be whipped to the front wall.

Fourth Day. Spend the first half of the period repeating what you did the time before. Spend the last part of the period learning the *back wall shot.* Back wall play is one of the more important fundamentals of four-wall handball since, during the course of a game, many returns must be played off the back wall. The most difficult part of back wall play is moving to the proper position to play the ball. The height and speed at which the balls rebound from the front wall determine how close to the back wall you must be in order to execute this return properly. Position yourself with feet parallel to the side wall. Turn your shoulders and head toward the back wall in order to watch the ball. Draw your arm back into the backswing position and let the ball drop as low as possible **using your low sidearm stroke to attempt the shot**. Shift the weight from your back foot to your front foot as you contact the ball with your arm on a line with the center of the body. Your full weight should be on your front foot at the end of the follow through. Figure 4.12 illustrates the proper form for the back wall return.

Back wall returns require timing that can only be gained through much practice. Begin by throwing the ball so it strikes the front wall, bounces on the floor, and hits the back wall. Move into position facing a side wall and catch the ball as it comes off the back wall. Do this several

Figure 4.12 Player hitting a back wall return: Note that shot is hit with the low sidearm stroke.

times and then stand about 8' from the back wall and toss the ball easily against the back wall so that it bounces on the floor toward the front wall. Move out with the ball using side steps so that your feet remain parallel with the side wall throughout the action. When the ball gets to a low position, plant your back foot and stride toward the front wall with your front foot as you catch the ball.

Next, stand in approximately the same position as before and bounce the ball to the floor so that it then strikes the back wall and rebounds toward the front wall. Move out with the ball as on the previous drill and attempt to catch the ball about knee high before it hits the floor. After you feel you are in the proper position when catching the ball, attempt to hit the ball as it comes off the back wall. Practice hitting this shot in the three drills described. Keep your eye on the ball, and remember the important point of contact.

The straight back wall return just described is the simplest of the back wall shots. One of the most difficult shots for the beginner is playing a ball that hits the floor, then strikes a side wall and continues to the back wall. This is the ball that "*comes around the corner*," as illustrated in Figure 4.13. If you are right-handed, you should face the left rear corner and pivot following the ball and attempt the shot with your right hand. This around-the-corner back wall return is illustrated in Figure 4.14. Again, the low sidearm stroke is the one to use. If you are left-handed, you should not pivot but back up and play the ball off the back wall with your left hand. Of course, do just the opposite on balls that come around the right rear corner.

Fifth Day. Repeat during the first half of this period what you did the previous day. Every time you enter a court, begin by throwing the ball. Next, drop the ball to the floor and stroke your shot. Next, toss the ball to the front wall and practice making returns from all parts of the court with your various arm strokes, with particular emphasis on your weaknesses.

Today, have another player in the court so you can participate in a "serving and receiving drill." (See Rules 4.1, 4.5, and 4.6 in Chapter 3 on serves.) One player serves the ball ten times, five with the right hand and five with the left. The receiver stands halfway between the side walls and two steps from the back wall. Remember the ready position discussed earlier. When the server hits a legal serve, move to the ball and attempt your return (see Rule 4.7 on return of serve). Whether or not you make a legal return, stop the action and let the server serve again. After one player has served ten times and the other player has attempted the returns, switch positions and continue the drill for the remainder of the period.

Figure 4.13 Ball "coming around the rear corner."

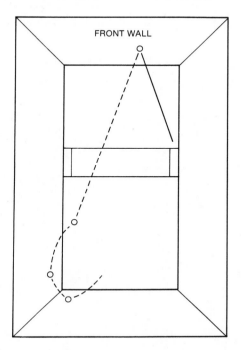

Sixth Day. Study the rules carefully before beginning today. Repeat the warm-up drill, practicing all of the various shots. Light stretching calisthenics should be included in your warm-up. After about 15 minutes, start the game. Don't worry about winning or losing, but concentrate on watching the ball, moving into proper position, and using the proper arm stroke.

Points to Remember

1. Master the basic arm strokes.
2. Face the side wall when attempting your shot.
3. Don't rush your shot. Wait until the ball has reached the top of its bounce and is dropping before attempting the hit.
4. Stride toward the front wall on all shot attempts.

Figure 4.14 Player hitting a back wall return "coming around" the left rear corner: Note that player begins by facing the rear corner, then pivots and attempts shot with the low sidearm stroke.

5. Remember the point of contact, on a line with the center of the body.

6. Don't take a cramped swing.

7. Don't try to hit the ball as hard as you can.

8. Be aggressive. Start moving into position as soon as the ball leaves your opponent's hand.

9. Don't ignore your weak hand, but practice hard to overcome the weakness.

10. Keep your eye on the ball at all times.

11. Hit the back wall return with the low sidearm stroke.

The Serves

The serve is the most important shot in the game of handball. A player can score a point only when serving, so he should not serve merely to put the ball into play but should attempt his best possible serve to force a weak return from his opponent.

A beginner may not realize the importance of a well-placed serve because an inexperienced opponent will have difficulty returning any kind of serve. As his opponents improve, however, he will find it very difficult to hit a serve that isn't returned. Most serves—even the very good ones—can be returned, but just how well they are returned depends upon their being properly executed and directed toward the opponent's weakness. The importance of mastering a variety of good serves cannot be overemphasized.

BASIC SERVES

The basic serves should be mastered by all players. Most of them should be directed to the opponent's nondominant hand. All serves that can be hit toward the left rear corner can also be directed toward the right rear corner if an opponent happens to be left-handed.

Low Drive Serve

To hit a low drive serve, use the low sidearm stroke that was discussed in Chapter 4. Stand in the rear of the service zone with your feet set fairly close together so you can take a long stride forward when making contact with the ball. Flex your knees and bend at the waist. Hold the ball in the opposite hand from the one you will use to hit the serve, and drop the ball to the floor from about the height of the knees and far enough in front of the body so that you can meet the ball with your natural sidearm stroke. Wait until the ball has reached the top of its bounce and is starting to drop before making contact. Hit the serve very hard and low against the front wall so that the ball will stay low on the rebound and bounce just across the short line angling toward one of the rear corners. Figure 5.1 illustrates a player executing a low drive serve.

Try to picture an imaginary line parallel to and about 6' behind the short line. Your low drive serve should rebound from the front wall and bounce on the floor between the short line and this imaginary line. If you attempt to hit this serve from a higher position, it will usually rebound from the front wall too high and bounce too deep in the court, thus giving your opponent the opportunity to hit a back wall return. None of your serves should be playable off the back wall.

The low drive serve should not hit a side wall but should be angled so it will stay close to a side wall when rebounding toward the rear corner. (See Fig. 5.2.) This will force your opponent to attempt his return with his nondominant hand from a position very deep in the rear court and close to the side wall.

This serve can be executed from several positions along the service zone, but most good players stand about halfway between the side walls, so they will have the opportunity of serving the ball toward either rear corner. Do not stand too near a side wall when attempting to serve the ball along that same side wall. This would constitute a screen ball. (See Rule 4.4 b.)

Changeup Serve

The difference between the changeup serve and the low drive serve is in height and speed. The ball is served from approximately a waist high position with a half-speed sidearm stroke. It is a change-of-pace serve that hits the front wall higher than does the low drive serve, but it is hit easier so that it will rebound and bounce on the floor between the short line and

Figure 5.1   Player hitting the low drive serve: Note short step of right foot (back foot) to begin forward motion, and long stride of left foot just before contact with ball.

Figure 5.2   The low drive serve: Note that ball strikes floor close to the short line to keep from rebounding off the back wall.

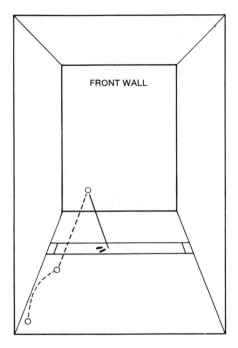

FRONT WALL

the imaginary line 6′ behind the short line, as did the low drive serve. This serve should also be angled so that it stays close to the side wall and does not rebound off the back wall.

Try to hit the changeup serve at a speed and height that will force your opponent to attempt his return from a height between his waist and shoulders.

Lob Serve

The lob serve can be executed with either the underarm stroke or the overhand stroke. Figure 5.3 illustrates the form for the overhand lob serve. The ball should strike the front wall very high, but it must be hit softly in order to make it drop steeply after hitting the front wall and bounce on the floor just behind the short line. After striking the floor, it should take a high bounce and then drop into the rear corner, striking the back wall very low. (See Fig. 5.4.) If the server is trying to place the ball into the left rear corner, he should stand 3 or 4′ from the left side wall and

Figure 5.3 Player hitting the lob serve with overhand stroke: Note that server is very close to left side wall when serving to the left rear corner.

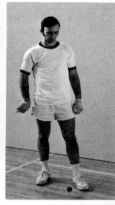

Figure 5.4 The lob serve: Note that ball strikes floor just behind short line and remains close to side wall while angling to left rear corner.

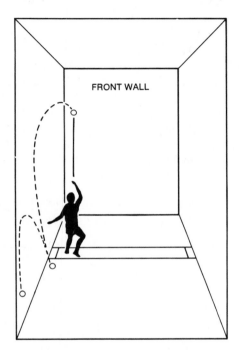

angle this soft lob serve so it remains close to the side wall all the way back to the rear corner.

Properly hit, this serve will force the opponent to attempt his return with an overhand stroke using his nondominant hand.

Z-Serve

The **Z-Serve** is sometimes called a **three-wall serve** or a **scotch twist serve**. It can be executed by using either the sidearm or the overhand stroke. If the server is attempting to place his serve in the left rear corner, he should stand a few inches away from the left side wall and hit the ball against the front wall about 2′ from the right side wall. After contacting the front wall the ball then strikes the right side wall and angles across the court toward the left rear corner. The serve should hit the front wall high enough for the ball to strike the floor about halfway between the short line and the back wall, and it should then hit the left side wall about 2' from the back wall. (See Fig. 5.5.)

When the Z-serve strikes the front wall and the right side wall, the ball develops a counterclockwise spin. When the ball bounces from the floor and strikes the left side wall, this spin will cause the ball to rebound from the left side wall almost parallel with the back wall. It is important that the ball not rebound off the back wall high enough for a back wall return.

The Z-serve must be hit hard so that the ball will cross diagonally in front of the receiver to his nondominant hand. If this serve is hit too gently, the receiver will have time to move up and hit the ball before it bounces on the floor, and he will be able to use his strong hand.

Figure 5.5 The Z-serve: Note that server is very near side wall, and ball strikes close to the corner of the front wall.

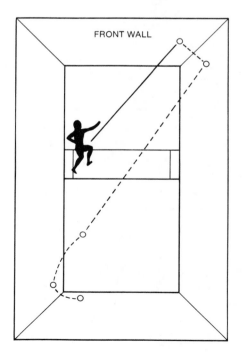

A right-handed player will find it very easy to hit a Z-serve into the right rear corner but more difficult to hit it toward the left rear corner. Remember, you want the receiver to attempt the return with his nondominant hand.

ADVANCED SERVES

After you have mastered the basic serves, experiment with the more advanced serves. Most good players have perfected at least one advanced serve that can be used if their basic serves are not achieving good results. This does not mean that you cannot serve effectively using only the basic serves. However, the greater your variety of serves, the more likely that you will be able to find an opponent's weakness.

Hook Serves

The hook serve, sometimes called a **hop serve,** is projected in the same direction as the low drive serve and the changeup serve, but a spin (or English) is applied to the ball when the serve is made. This spin causes the ball to break sharply to the left or right after rebounding from the front wall and striking the floor. The hook that breaks to the left when hit by the right hand is called a *natural hook*, and the hook that breaks to the right when hit by the right hand is called a *reverse hook*. The opposite is true when the ball is hit with the left hand. The hook that breaks left is a reverse, and the hook that breaks right is a natural.

A hook ball must hit the front wall first, rebound, and strike the floor before making contact with another wall. If, after hitting the front wall, the ball hits another wall before striking the floor, the spin will be neutralized, and the hook will not occur.

Natural Hook. The arm motion used in the execution of a natural hook is similar to the sidearm stroke, but instead of pointing your forearm and fingers toward the side wall, they should point down toward the floor when making contact with the ball. Hold your hand in a natural cup with the thumb lined up in front of the index finger, as shown in Figure 5.7. Contact the ball in the palm of the hand and rotate the hand and forearm inward when releasing the shot, so the ball will roll across and spin off the palm and thumb in a clockwise rotation. Keep your elbow close to your abdomen when contacting the ball and on the follow-through arm motion. This arm motion is similar to a baseball pitcher's when he is throwing a

Figure 5.6 (a) The natural hook angled to left rear corner (hit with the right hand). **(b)** The natural hook angled to the right rear corner (hit with the right hand): Note that ball "straightens out" parallel to the side wall.

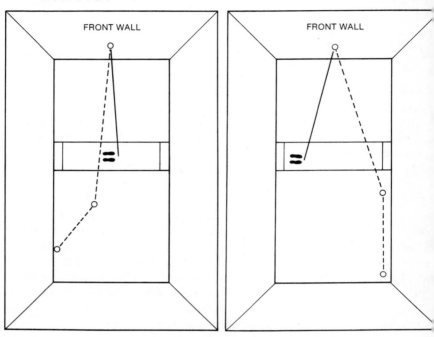

Figure 5.7 Hand position for hitting the natural hook: Note that thumb lines up in front of the first finger.

curve, except that the ball is contacted from about the height of the knees. Figure 5.8 illustrates the correct way to hit a natural hook.

It takes a lot of spin to make the ball hook, so immediately after making the initial contact with the ball, rotate your hand and forearm rapidly in order to apply the needed spin.

Reverse Hook. The reverse hook is the opposite of the natural hook and is more difficult to execute because the arm stroke used is not a natural throwing motion. Contact should be made from about the height of the knees. Hold your hand in a natural cup with the forearm and fingers pointing toward the floor when you contact the ball. Make initial contact with the ball at about the point where the index finger joins the palm. Rotate your forearm and hand outward in a counterclockwise motion to make the ball roll across your hand and spin off where the little finger and

Figure 5.8 Player hitting the natural hook: Note that elbow and hand rotate inward to apply clockwise spin on ball.

the palm join. This wrapping motion will cause the ball to spin counterclockwise as it leaves the hand. Figure 5.10 illustrates correct form in hitting a reverse hook.

Points to remember

1. It's not how hard you hit the ball that makes it hook, but the spin applied when the hand and forearm rotate sharply.
2. Underspin or overspin on the ball will not cause it to hook. Make sure the ball is low enough when making contact with the hand so that your forearm and fingers point toward the floor.
3. The ball should be fairly close to your body when contact is made. This will make it easier for the hand to "cut" the ball on

Figure 5.9 (a) The reverse hook angled to right rear corner (hit with the right hand). **(b)** The reverse hook angled to left rear corner (hit with the right hand).

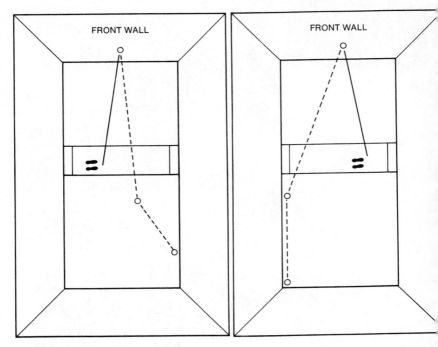

Figure 5.10 Player hitting the reverse hook: Note that elbow and hand rotate outward to apply counter-clockwise spin on ball.

the inside (natural hook) or "wrap" the ball on the outside (reverse hook). Also, the closer the ball is to your body, the more difficult it is for your opponent to see what type of spin you are applying.

4. Because hitting a hook requires a very sharp twist of the forearm, make sure that your arms are well warmed up before attempting this shot, or you might develop a sore arm.

Like the low drive serve and the changeup serve, the hook serve should rebound toward the rear corner without hitting the side or back wall. If you are a right-handed player, the natural hook should strike the floor several feet from the left side wall (depending on how much of a break your hook usually takes) so the ball will break left into the rear corner. The reverse hook should bounce close to the left side wall so it will straighten out and stay close to the side wall all the way back to the rear corner. Of course, the opposite is true if you are attempting to execute a hook serve toward the right rear corner.

Even after you have learned to hit the ball so it will hook, it still takes a great deal of practice to control this shot. Remember, the effectiveness of any shot depends upon your ability to control its placement.

Crotch Serve

The **crotch** serve requires a high degree of accuracy and a certain element of luck. This serve is hit low and hard like a low drive serve, and it is angled so the ball strikes the juncture of the side wall and floor just after crossing the short line. (See Fig. 5.11.) If this serve is executed perfectly, the ball will roll out after hitting the crotch, thus allowing no return. There is a greater chance of the ball rolling out of the left side wall crotch if a natural hook spin (hit by the right hand) is applied to the serve. Reverse hook spin (hit by the right hand) should be applied if you are trying to hit the right side wall crotch with your serve.

This is a dangerous serve, because if the ball misses the crotch it will most often rebound off the side wall to the middle of the court, thus allowing the receiver to make an easy return.

Figure 5.11 The crotch serve: Note that ball contacts side wall just above floor.

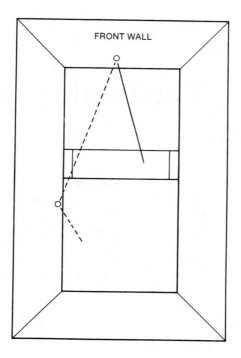

The Basic Shots

After you have mastered the basic hitting strokes and you are able to judge the different court angles well enough to get into good position for your shot attempts, begin practicing the basic shots. There are four shots in handball, the mastery of which is considered basic to the game. These basic shots are (1) *the kill,* (2) *the pass,* (3) *the ceiling,* and (4) *the three wall.* The kill and the pass are offensive shots, and the ceiling and three wall are defensive shots.

OFFENSIVE SHOTS

Offensive shots are hit with the purpose of ending the rally. They are hit at such a height, angle, or speed that the opponent cannot reach the ball in time to make a legal return.

There are three ways you can win a rally: (1) if you hit a kill shot, (2) if you hit a pass shot, or (3) if your opponent makes an error. A beginner wins most rallies by his opponents' mistakes. However, as your skill and that of your opponents improve, these mistakes become less frequent, and one of the offensive kill or pass shots is necessary to win a rally.

The Kill Shot

The most spectacular of all the handball shots and the most difficult to execute is the kill shot. This is the offensive shot that strikes the front wall very near the floor and rebounds so low that the opponent cannot make a legal return. The kill shot requires great accuracy because the ball must strike the front wall dangerously close to the floor. Of course, if your attempted kill shot hits the floor before striking the front wall, you lose the rally.

There are two types of kill shots, the *straight kill* and the *corner kill.* The particular type of kill shot you should attempt depends upon the court position of your opponent. Kill shot strategy is discussed in Chapter 7.

Straight Kill. The straight kill shot strikes the front wall very low and rebounds without striking another wall. (See Fig. 6.1.) The most effective straight kill shots remain close to a side wall on the rebound.

Figure 6.1 The straight kill shot.

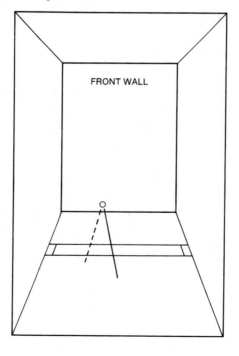

FRONT WALL

Corner Kill. All corner kill shots strike two walls before contacting the floor. They can sometimes strike the first wall a little higher than a straight kill because the ball may lose some of its height when angling toward the second wall. The ball should strike the second wall very low, as in the straight kill shot. There are four basic corner kill shots.

Right Inside Corner Kill. The right inside corner kill shot contacts the front wall first and then strikes the right side wall very low before contacting the floor. (See Fig. 6.2.)

Right Outside Corner Kill. The right outside corner kill shot first contacts the right side wall and then strikes the front wall very low before rebounding toward the left side wall. (See Fig. 6.3.)

Left Inside Corner Kill. The left inside corner kill shot first contacts the front wall and then strikes the left side wall very low before contacting the floor. (See Fig. 6.4.)

Figure 6.2 The right inside corner kill shot: Note that ball hits front wall first.

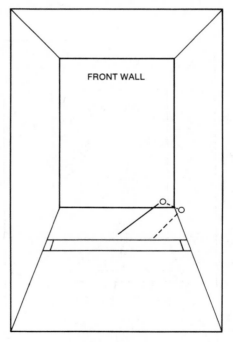

Left Outside Corner Kill. The left outside corner kill shot contacts the left side wall first and then strikes the front wall very low before rebounding toward the right side wall. (See Fig. 6.5.)

Kill shots are especially difficult for the beginning player because he tends to rush his shots and usually contacts the ball above his waist. Attempting a kill shot from such a high position is foolish for two reasons: (1) the player will have to change the downward angle of his shot as he stands closer to or further from the front wall, and (2) even if he is fortunate enough to hit his shot low against the front wall, the rebound of the ball will bounce high on the floor because of the angle of projection of the shot. The kill shot must rebound taking low bounces so that the opponent will not be able to make the retrieve.

It is important in the execution of the kill shot to learn to wait for the ball to drop to a low position. The lower you contact the ball with

Figure 6.3 The right outside corner kill shot: Note that ball hits side wall first.

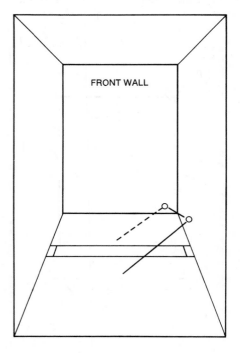

FRONT WALL

your low sidearm stroke, the better the chances of your shot hitting low against the front wall. This low position will not be the same for every player. You must experiment to see how low you can contact the ball and yet not be off balance. Knee height is a good position, although many players can comfortably contact the ball at a lower level.

The follow-through arm motion is also important. Contact the ball with the forearm parallel with the floor and the fingers pointing toward the side wall, as illustrated in Figure 6.6. Remain in your low crouched position on the follow-through arm motion so that the forearm remains level throughout the stroke. (See Fig. 6.7.) Often a player attempting a kill shot contacts the ball at the proper low height but makes the mistake of straightening to an upright position on his follow through. This usually causes the ball to rise on its trajectory to the front wall. The low contact and low-level follow through are essential if the kill shot is to be executed properly and consistently.

Figure 6.4 The left inside corner kill shot: Note that ball hits front wall first.

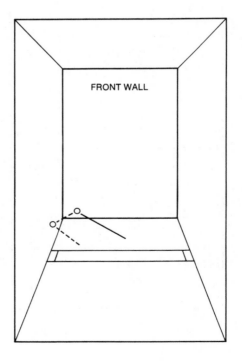

Practicing the Kill Shot. You must become accustomed to flexing the knees and bending at the waist in order to be in a low position when attempting a kill shot. Begin by standing in the service area, bending over into the low crouched position, and throw the ball low against the front wall with your low sidearm stroke. Try to make the ball hit the front wall about 6″ from the floor or lower. Next, bend over and drop the ball to the floor from about knee high. Allow the ball to reach the top of its bounce and begin its descent before attempting to hit the ball with your low sidearm stroke. Remember to swing level and stay down on your follow through.

Next, stand just behind the short line and toss the ball very gently so that it strikes the front wall about 4′ from the floor. As soon as you release the ball, move into position and get set to attempt your kill shot. Allow the ball to drop to the lowest possible height before stepping into

Figure 6.5 The left outside corner kill shot: Note that ball hits side wall first.

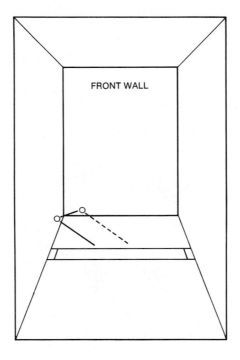

Figure 6.6 Position for attempting the kill shot using low sidearm stroke: Note that forearm is parallel to floor.

Figure 6.7 Follow-through position after attempting the kill shot: Note that player remains in low crouch and forearm is parallel to floor.

the shot and making contact with the ball. Continue practicing by tossing the ball to the front wall gently so it rebounds at different angles and move quickly into position to attempt the kill shot.

When you can consistently hit low shots from the front court, move further back and attempt kill shots from deeper court positions. Also, practice hitting kill shots when attempting back wall returns. Use your same low sidearm stroke when attempting the back wall kill shot.

After you become consistent in hitting kill shots from all possible court positions, begin attempting to angle your kill shots so they will remain close to a side wall on the rebound. First practice these shots from the front court, and then gradually move further away from the front wall to attempt them.

Next, learn to execute the different corner kill shots by first practicing these shots from the front court then from deeper court positions, including attempts off the back wall.

Notice, when attempting corner kills, that if you hit the left wall first with a right-handed attempt, or if you hit the right wall first with a left-handed attempt, the ball must hit the side wall very close to the front wall in order for it to carry to the front wall. This is because of the spin of the ball when it leaves your hand.

Points to Remember

1. Move into position and get set before attempting your shot.
2. Don't rush your shot.
3. Contact the ball as near to the floor as comfortably possible.
4. Attempt your kill shot with the low sidearm stroke.
5. Remain in a crouched position on your follow-through arm motion.
6. Learn to execute kill shots from all possible court positions.
7. Learn to hit corner kills as well as straight kills.
8. Don't try to hit perfect rollout kill shots.

The Pass Shot

The offensive pass shot is so called because it is driven past the opponent. Whenever you are unsure which shot to attempt, a pass shot angled toward the rear corner of your opponent's weak hand is usually a good choice. The pass shot can be hit with the overhand stroke, the sidearm stroke, and the low sidearm stroke with the cupped hand. It can also be hit with the underhand stroke, using the closed fist.

To be effective the pass shot must (1) hit the front wall first, (2) be hit hard (or else the opponent will have time to reach it), (3) be angled so that it will rebound out of the opponent's reach, and (4) be hit low enough so that the ball will die as it gets to the back wall. Hitting the pass shot too high will allow your opponent the opportunity for a back wall return.

The pass shot is most effective if the opponent is in front court or if he is near a side wall in rear court. It is impossible to pass an opponent who is in the middle of the back court. For this reason, the best pass shots are usually hit with the low sidearm stroke—the same stroke used in the execution of the kill shot. Hitting the ball from this height will cause the opponent to move to the front court in order to anticipate a possible kill shot.

There are two types of pass shots, the *straight pass* and the *two-wall pass.*

Straight Pass. The straight pass shot first strikes the front wall and then rebounds toward a rear corner without hitting another wall. (See Fig. 6.8.)

Two-Wall Pass. The two-wall pass shots hit the front wall first and then strike a side wall a few feet behind the short line before bouncing on the floor. The ball should hit the side wall about 2′ from the floor and then rebound toward the back wall. (See Fig. 6.9.) This shot is usually angled to the left when hit by a player standing in the right half of the court and to the right when hit from the left half of the court.

Practicing the Pass Shot. Begin by standing in the front court and throwing the ball to the front wall at the proper angle so that it will rebound like a pass shot. Try to make your straight pass remain close to a side wall on its rebound. Next, drop the ball to the floor and attempt to hit a straight pass down either wall. Then attempt a two-wall pass down either wall. Next, toss the ball to the front wall so that it will rebound at different angles and different heights, and attempt the pass shots with your various arm strokes. Gradually move deeper in the court and practice these shots from all court positions. Also practice hitting the different passing shots on your back wall return.

Points to Remember

1. Power is essential for the execution of the pass shot. Get into good position so you can stride toward the front wall when attempting this shot.

2. Learn the two types of pass shots with both hands.
3. Keep the pass shot from rebounding off the back wall.
4. Practice the pass shot from all areas of the court with your various arm strokes.

Fly Kill and Fly Pass Shots

The various fly kill and fly pass shots are the same as the kill and pass shots previously discussed, except they are attempted before the ball contacts the floor. These very important offensive shots are difficult to execute because there is little time to get set before attempting them.

These shots are usually hit by a player in the front court. A player should very seldom try one of these shots from a rear court position. It is easier to let a ball in deep court bounce and attempt your shot as it is rebounding off the back wall.

Practice the various fly kill and fly pass shots by standing a couple of feet behind the short line and tossing the ball high and easy to the front

Figure 6.8 The straight pass shot.

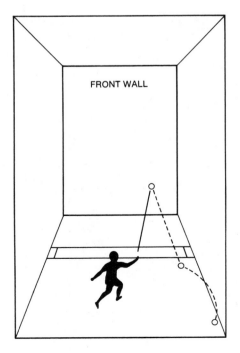

wall. Let the ball drop as low as possible before making contact with your low sidearm stroke. You can sometimes use the waist high sidearm stroke if you are attempting a corner kill shot because the ball will lose some of its height after hitting the first wall and will hit low on the second wall, especially if it is stroked softly. The ball should rarely be hit on the fly with the overhand stroke.

Also practice your fly shots by tossing the ball high into a front corner so that it first strikes the front wall and then a side wall before rebounding toward the center of the court. Always watch for this particular fly shot, because if you allow the ball to bounce on the floor at this angle, you will have to retreat to a difficult position in a rear corner to make your return attempt.

Do not attempt these fly shots if you are off balance or in poor position. In these cases it is better to retreat quickly and play the ball after the bounce.

Figure 6.9 The two-wall pass shot: Note that ball contacts the side wall just behind the short line.

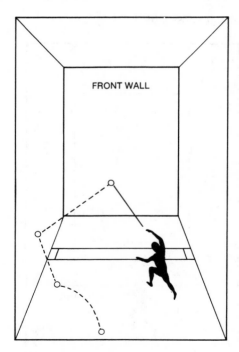

DEFENSIVE SHOTS

A defensive shot is hit in order to move your opponent into a rear court position as close to the back wall as possible. Your opponent will probably be able to return the shot, but it will be difficult for him to hit an offensive shot from that deep in the court. Attempt a defensive shot whenever you do not have a good chance of hitting one of the offensive kill or pass shots. The defensive shot can also give you time to move up into front center court while your opponent is retreating to the rear court.

There are two basic defensive shots: (1) the *ceiling shot,* and (2) the *three-wall shot.*

Ceiling Shot

The ceiling shot is a defensive shot projected so that it strikes the ceiling before contacting the front wall. The ball should hit the ceiling at a distance of from 1' to 4' from the front wall. It will then drop steeply to the floor and take a very high bounce to the rear of the court. (See Fig. 6.10.) If the ball hits the ceiling too far from the front wall, it will hit the floor before striking the front wall. If a ceiling shot is hit too hard, it will rebound too high, thus allowing your opponent an opportunity for a back wall return. A correctly executed shot will strike the back wall too low for a back wall return attempt.

Figure 6.10 The ceiling shot.

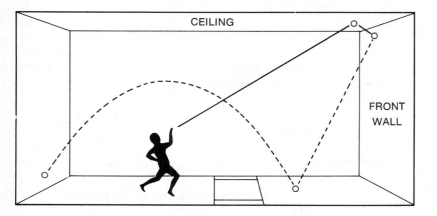

The ceiling shot can be executed by using one of two strokes. Whenever the ball must be contacted at a shoulder high or higher level, a ceiling shot is usually the correct choice of shots. This shot is hit with the overhand arm stroke, as illustrated in Figure 6.11. As with the other basic shots, get in a set position and shift your weight from your back foot forward to your front foot as you contact the ball.

The ceiling shot can also be executed by contacting the ball below the waist, using the underhand stroke with the closed fist, as illustrated in Figure 6.12. Face the side wall, bend your knees, and stride into the shot. Contact the ball on the upswing of your underhand stroke, and straighten your legs on the follow-through motion. The ball should contact the fist on the cuticle area, as shown in Figure 6.13. The fist ceiling shot is not easy to control because of the smaller hitting surface of the fist as compared with the open hand. However, it is an important shot to learn because you will be able to hit a ceiling shot no matter what the height of the ball's bounce.

Stand in the rear third of the court to practice. Most ceiling shots during a game are attempted from this area. Throw the ball high against the front wall so that it will rebound deep in the court. Position yourself so you can step into the ball using your three-quarter speed overhand stroke. Notice how deep in the court your shot travels. If it hits over 4' from the floor on the back wall, you should hit your next attempt with less power. If your shot does not reach the back wall, hit your next attempt slightly harder. Also throw ceiling shots and attempt ceiling shot returns.

Practice your underhand fist ceiling shot on balls thrown high and easy and also on balls thrown to rebound like the low drive serve. Again, notice where your shots end up, and adjust the force of your stroke accordingly.

When you can hit ceiling shots consistently at the proper speed, then try to angle your shots so they will drop into one of the rear corners. This is one of the best shots in handball because it not only drives the opponent into the rear court but also places him in a difficult rear corner position for his return attempt.

Points to Remember

1. Always position yourself so you can step toward the front wall as you contact the ball.
2. Hit the ceiling shot from above the waist with the open hand or from below the waist with the closed fist.

Figure 6.11 Hitting the ceiling shot with the overhand stroke: Note that right shoulder is lower than left at the beginning of the stroke.

Figure 6.12 Hitting the ceiling shot with the underhand stroke: Note that shot is hit with the fist.

Figure 6.13 Hand position for the fist shot: Note where ball contacts fist.

3. Do not hit the ceiling shot so hard that it allows the opponent an opportunity for a back wall return.
4. Learn to angle your ceiling shots into the rear corners.
5. Practice your ceiling shots from the rear third of the court. The ceiling shot is rarely attempted from a front court position or on a back wall return.

Three-Wall Shot

The three-wall shot is the defensive shot that hits three walls before bouncing on the floor and rebounding into a rear corner. As illustrated in Figure 6.14, the ball first hits a side wall before contacting the front wall.

Figure 6.14 The three-wall shot that first hits the right side wall: Note where ball contacts front wall (compare to the high Z-serve, Fig. 6.15).

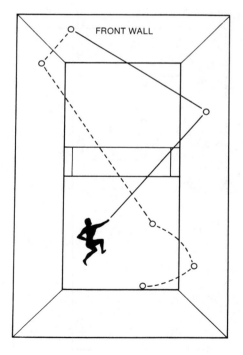

After it hits the front wall, it strikes the other side wall and rebounds, landing on the floor approximately 8′ behind the short line. It then strikes the side wall about 4′ from the back wall.

Hit this shot so that the ball will contact the side wall about 15′ from the floor. If the shot is hit at the proper angle and speed, it will contact the front wall very close to the opposite side wall at approximately the same height. Thus, if your shot first hits the right side wall, it will rebound toward the right rear corner much like a high Z-serve angled in that direction. (See Fig. 6.15.) It is important that your shot contact the front wall at approximately the point indicated in the illustration. Should your shot contact the front wall closer to the center, the ball will probably rebound off the back wall which would, of course, be a poor shot.

Figure 6.15 The high Z-serve: Note similarities of the rebound to the three-wall shot. Ball contacts right side wall after bouncing on floor.

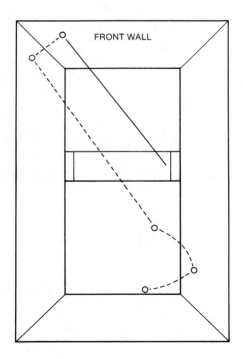

To be effective, the three-wall shot must be hit very hard. If it is hit too gently, the ball will not carry deep enough in the court, and your opponent will have an opportunity for a fly shot in center court.

If your three-wall shot attempt is going to hit the right side wall first, the ball should have a clockwise spin when it leaves your hand. Therefore, this shot can be hit with the right hand sidearm stroke, and because the ball has the opposite spin when struck by the closed fist, it can also be hit with the left hand fist stroke. If your three-wall shot is going to hit the left side wall first, the ball should be spinning counterclockwise and can be hit with your left hand sidearm stroke or the right hand fist stroke. The direction of spin is important. If the ball is spinning clockwise when contacting the left side wall first or counterclockwise when contacting the right side wall first, the ball will slow down and not carry deep enough in the court to be effective.

Practice the three-wall shot from the rear third of the court. From the left rear corner of the court, the ball can be struck from any height with the right arm open hand stroke, but should be contacted waist high or lower with the left hand fist stroke. If the ball must be hit with the left hand from a high position, the open hand ceiling shot is the correct attempt. Of course, the opposite applies when the three-wall shot is attempted from the right rear corner.

Points to Remember

1. The three-wall shot hits a side wall first and then contacts the front wall and the opposite side wall before bouncing on the floor.
2. The shot should rebound like a high Z-serve, striking a rear side wall after bouncing on the floor.
3. The shot should be hit very hard.
4. If the shot contacts the right side wall first, use the right hand sidearm stroke with the open hand or the left hand fist stroke. The opposite applies if the ball hits the left side wall first.
5. The shot is usually hit from the rear third of the court.

Strategy of Singles Play

Someone once wrote, *"A man who uses his hand only is called a laborer. A man who uses his head only is an apprentice, but a man who uses his hand, head, and heart is an artist."* Learning how to hit the ball where you want it is obviously important. But learning how to think while playing and how to choose the correct shot for a particular situation is the artistry of the game. This chapter is devoted to shot choice—the strategy of handball singles.

THE SERVE

The player who controls the front court usually wins the rally. When a player is serving, he not only has the all-important front court position, but he also has his opponent in a very poor position in deep court. When you are serving, don't use the serve simply as a means of putting the ball into play. Rather, utilize your opponent's weakness to force a weak return which will allow you to keep your front court position. If you can maintain this position after the serve, you will probably win the rally, because it is much easier to hit an offensive shot from the front court than from the rear court.

The best serve is the one that is the most effective against a particular opponent. Since players have different strengths and weaknesses, and a serve that works very well against one player might be handled very easily by another player, the importance of mastering a variety of good serves cannot be overemphasized. You should learn to execute all the serves discussed in Chapter 5. Most serves should accomplish three objectives against all opponents: (1) They should be directed toward the opponent's nondominant hand. Very few serves should be angled toward a player's strong hand, although good handball players occasionally try to surprise their opponent by hitting a low drive serve to his strong hand. (2) They should be angled to stay close to the side wall when rebounding toward the rear corner. The closer the ball is to the side wall, the further the receiver will have to move to get into a position to make the return and the less time he will have to get set. (3) They should be hit at such a height and speed that the ball will not rebound off of the back wall. Don't let the back wall neutralize your serve by giving your opponent time to get in a good position for his return.

A good server in handball is much like a good pitcher in baseball. All great pitchers have one thing in common—good control—and most also have mastery of a good variety of pitches. A good server in handball must also have good control in the placement of his serves. Control is more important than power. If you cannot control your hard low drive serve, it is better to hit the ball with less power and be able to place your shots accurately.

Try to keep the receiver off balance by not only varying the angle and height of your serves but also by occasionally varying the speed. Sometimes, after having given your opponent a steady diet of low drive serves, a changeup or lob serve might get you an easy point.

If you don't know your opponent's particular strengths and weaknesses, you should "feel him out." Serve every good serve you know how to hit, and watch how he reacts to the different angles, heights, and speeds. After a few points, it should become fairly obvious what types of serves he has the most difficulty returning, and you should use those serves throughout most of the game. If you discover that a particular serve is giving the receiver a tough time, continue that serve until he begins to handle it easier and then switch to another serve.

If you properly execute the low drive serve, your opponent will be forced to attempt his return from around knee high. The properly hit changeup serve will cause him to attempt his return from a waist high position, and the lob serve will cause a return attempt from a shoulder high or higher position. You cannot determine the strength of a player's weak hand by watching him hit just one shot. Some players have a very strong nondominant hand from a low position and are weaker when the ball must be struck from a higher position. Find out which height gives your opponent the most difficulty.

If your opponent returns your serve, you naturally want him to return it to your strong hand. When the ball is very close to a side wall, he will have a hard time returning the ball so that it will rebound down that same wall. He is more likely to put his return down the opposite side. If you are right-handed, your good low drive, changeup and lob serves angled down the left wall will often cause your opponent to return the ball to your right hand. If you assume the position shown in Figure 7.1, your good Z-serve will also force the receiver's return to your right hand, because he cannot return the serve back down the left wall unless it is a high defensive return.

Remember that when serving you have 10 seconds in which to put the ball into play. Don't be in a hurry. Take your time and decide which

Figure 7.1 Arrow points to position right-handed player should assume after Z-serve: Note that this position "blocks" a pass or kill shot attempt down the left wall.

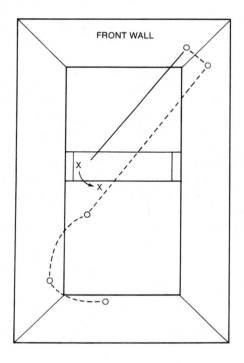

serve will be the most effective against your opponent. This is the only time in the game when you can stand still, relax, and hit the ball when you are ready, so decide exactly where you want your serve to go and then hit your shot to that exact spot.

THE RETURN OF SERVICE

As mentioned earlier, the server has the advantage and the receiver is at a disadvantage because of their court positions. The receiver must attempt to neutralize the server's advantage with a strong return of serve. It is very difficult to execute a good offensive shot when you are in the rear court, so be careful with your return. You don't want to allow the server to keep his front court position where it will be easy for him to score the point.

If your opponent makes a mistake with his serve and gives you a setup, then go ahead and attempt an offensive pass or kill shot. Otherwise, hit the kind of shot that will cause him to retreat to the rear court and will allow you time to move to the front court. This will be one of your defensive shots—either a ceiling shot or a three-wall return.

The best return of a good low drive serve or changeup serve is a fist ceiling shot or a fist three-wall return. You will have to attempt an overhand ceiling shot if your opponent serves you a good lob serve. However, many great players believe that the receiver should never let a lob serve hit the floor but should quickly move up and hit it on the fly, trying to drive a passing shot down the side wall furthest from the server. One advantage of cutting off the lob serve is that your shot attempt is closer to the front wall than it would be if you let the serve rebound into the rear corner.

Good hook serves can give the receiver trouble, especially if he starts his arm swing too quickly. If it is apparent that the server is hitting hook serves, do not turn your body to face a side wall too soon. Keep your body facing the front wall until you see whether the ball is breaking to the left or to the right, and then quickly turn and make your shot. If you position yourself one short step from the back wall instead of the normal two steps, you will have more time to get set for this serve. Watching the server's arm will help you anticipate which direction the ball is going to break. If his elbow is close to his body when he makes contact with the ball, you can usually expect a natural hook, and if his elbow rotates out away from his body, you can expect the ball to reverse. A good hook serve will usually force the receiver to attempt a fist ceiling shot or fist three-wall return.

STRATEGY AFTER THE SERVE

It is important to have a purpose for each shot you attempt. There are times when you may be trying your best simply to return a tough shot, but most of the time you will be in a position to choose one of several possibilities.

Every time you attempt a shot, try to do one of two things. Either try to end the rally by hitting the ball completely out of your opponent's reach with an offensive kill or pass shot, or attempt a ceiling shot or three-wall return which will move your opponent into a rear court position.

When should you attempt an offensive shot and when should you hit a defensive shot? Whenever you have enough time to get set before hitting your shot and whenever you can attempt that shot from a low position, attempt an offensive kill or pass shot. When you do not have time to get set or when you must attempt your shot from a high position, you should consider yourself on the defense and attempt one of the good defensive shots.

Offensive Shots. The particular offensive shot you choose to hit will depend upon the court position of your opponent. Play the percentages. If your attempted kill shot must be a perfect rollout shot in order for your opponent to miss the return, your shot placement is wrong. Aim your attempted kill shot so that if it is not a perfect shot it will still be a good shot angled away from your opponent. (The various types of kill shots were discussed in the preceding chapter.)

If you are attempting a kill shot from the front court and your opponent is in deep court, your best choice is a corner kill. If he is also nearer one side wall than the other, execute your corner kill by first hitting the side wall he is nearest. (See Fig. 7.2.) Even if you hit the shot a little high, the ball still ends up a long distance from your opponent.

When you attempt a kill shot from the rear court and your opponent has the front court position, try to hit a straight kill shot that will stay close to a side wall on its rebound. This shot should be hit very hard so that if it is not perfect, it may become a good pass shot. Your opponent will have to move to the side wall to attempt his return, and this will allow you to move up to front center court. If possible, attempt this shot down his weak hand side wall, although if you are close to the right wall, a shot

Figure 7.2 Best kill shot to attempt when opponent is in the rear court near a side wall: Note that ball first contacts the side wall nearest the opponent.

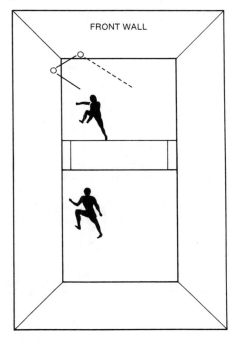

angled so that it will stay close to the right side wall on its rebound can be very effective because your opponent will often overplay the left side of the court in order to protect his weak hand. (See Fig. 7.3.)

If both you and your opponent are in front court, angle your kill shot so that when it rebounds your body will be between the ball and your opponent. Of course, whenever you have time to move out of your opponent's path to the ball, you must move, or an *avoidable hinder* will be called. (See Rule 4.11.) However, when you are close to the front wall and attempt a hard kill shot, you do not have time to move. If you accurately execute this kill shot, you will win the rally, and if you hit your shot too high, your opponent will be hindered. Either way is good strategy. Figure 7.4 illustrate the types of kill shots to attempt in these situations.

You cannot become a good handball player unless you can execute kill shots. If you don't have a good kill shot, your opponent can position himself deeper in the court when you are attempting your shot. It is

Figure 7.3 A straight kill shot hit by player standing near the right side wall and angled to remain near the right side wall on its rebound: Note that opponent is slightly "over-playing" the left side.

FRONT WALL

impossible to execute a rally-ending pass shot if your opponent is in the rear court (unless he is too close to one of the side walls). And if you can't hit a kill or pass shot, the only way you can win the rally is if your opponent makes an error. So you must learn to hit kill shots from all court positions. Whenever you attempt a shot from a low position, your opponent must move up close to the short line to have a chance at making the retrieve. When your opponent is near the short line, a well-executed pass shot can win the rally for you.

If you are closer to a side wall than your opponent and you attempt a pass shot that will rebound back down that same wall, you should use the straight pass shot. (See Fig. 7.5.) If you are attempting a pass shot down the opposite wall in the same situation, use the two-wall pass shot illustrated in Figure. 7.6. (The two types of pass shots were discussed in the preceding chapter.)

Figure 7.4 Best kill shots to attempt when both players are in front court: Note that ball angles away from opponent on rebound.

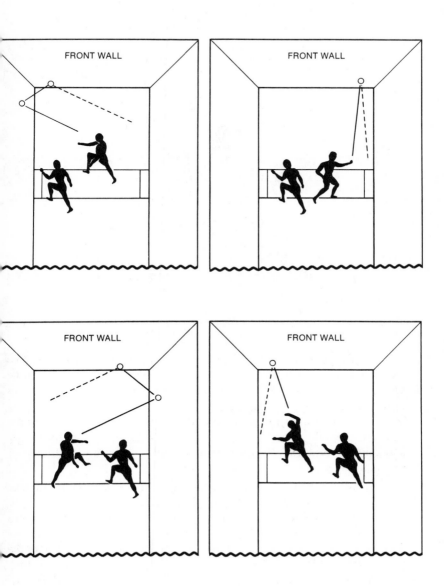

Figure 7.5 The straight pass shot: Note that ball rebounds close to side wall farthest from opponent.

A pass shot is considered safer than a kill shot. Even if your pass shot is not hit well enough to end the rally, your opponent will still be forced out of front court and will have to attempt his return from a less dangerous rear court position.

Attempting a fly kill or fly pass shot is always good strategy, because your opponent doesn't have as much time to gain good court position, and it is much easier to execute any scoring shot when your opponent is out of position.

Defensive Shots. When the percentages are against the execution of an offensive shot, attempt one of the defensive shots to move your opponent to a position close to the back wall and to give yourself time to move up to that important front court position. Notice that the defensive shots (discussed and illustrated in the preceding chapter) do not strike the front wall first, but strike either the ceiling or side wall before making contact with the front wall. *Unless you are attempting a rally-ending shot,*

Figure 7.6 The two-wall pass shot: Note that ball contacts the side wall just behind the opponent.

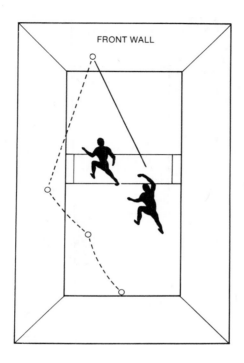

FRONT WALL

do not hit the front wall first. If you make the mistake of hitting the front wall first, and your shot is not a low kill or a pass shot rebounding close to a side wall, it will usually come to your opponent in center court. Thus, your court position will not be good, and he will have a good opportunity to hit an offensive shot.

Ideally, your defensive shot should not only force your opponent into the rear court to return the shot, but it should also force him to attempt his return with his weak hand. If your ceiling shot is angled so that it will drop into the weak hand rear corner, as illustrated in Figure 7.7, you might force a weak return that will result in a setup for you. A good defensive shot that forces your opponent into a mistake is very important. Sometimes, when a ceiling shot drops into the rear corner and is very close to the side wall, a so-called defensive shot may become an offensive shot too tough for your opponent to return.

Figure 7.7   The best angle for a ceiling shot: Note that ball drops into rear corner.

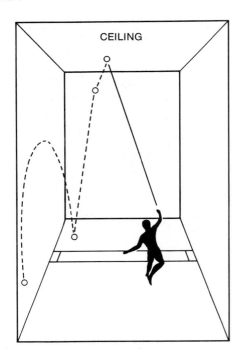

The three-wall return is a good defensive shot. However, there is a danger that your opponent may attempt to cut off the ball as it is rebounding across the court. If he is successful, lower the height of your shot and project it so that it first strikes the side wall very close to the front wall. This will cause the ball to rebound from the front wall and strike the other side wall very low and just behind the short line. Figure 7.8 illustrates that this angle will place the ball out of the opponent's reach in front court. If the shot is higher, it will rebound to the rear corner too high, thus allowing your opponent an opportunity for a back wall return.

WEAK HAND STRATEGY

Whenever you have a choice between hitting a shot with your weak hand or taking a few extra steps to get into position to use your strong

Figure 7.8 The low three-wall return: Note that ball contacts right side wall close to corner, and the angle of rebound is similar to the two-wall pass shot.

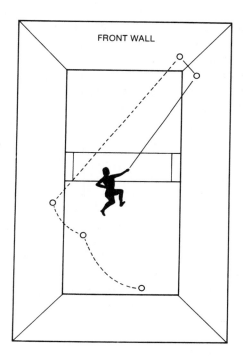

hand, always take the extra steps and hit the shot with your strong hand. You have a better chance of good execution with your strong hand. However, do not take the shot with your strong hand if you do not have time or room to take a comfortable and natural arm stroke. A shot hit by the weak hand from a good position is more accurate than one hit by the strong hand from a cramped or uncomfortable position. Most weak hand shots must be attempted from within about 4' of the left side wall, (if you are right-handed) so concentrate your practice of weak hand returns from this area.

What kinds of shots should you be able to execute with your weak hand? It would, of course, be good if you could hit all of the basic offensive and defensive shots, but this is not absolutely necessary. You can be a very good player without ever hitting an offensive shot with your weak hand. You must, however, be able to execute the defensive shots—especially the ceiling shot from above the waist with the open hand and from below the waist with the closed fist. Perhaps the greatest of all National Handball champions was **Jimmy Jacobs**. He won many of his titles using what he called his "sword and shield theory." His left hand was his shield. It was strictly defensive. Every time he hit a ball with it, his opponent was forced into a deep court position. His right hand was his sword. With this hand he executed his offensive shots. Of course Jacobs had the physical stamina and great control to play this type of game successfully—a more conservative game than that played by some of the other great players.

This is not to say that you should not try to develop offensive shots with your weak hand. Certainly, practice these shots, and if you learn to execute them with good consistency, then incorporate them into your game. Even an imperfect offensive kill shot hit when you are in the front court and your opponent is in the rear court will be difficult for your opponent to return because of his poor court position. But an offensive kill shot attempted from the rear court with your weak hand when the opponent is in good front court position is foolish, because you must hit a perfect shot in order to win the rally.

If you must hit the front wall first when attempting a weak hand return from the rear court, angle your shot like a passing shot. Figure 7.9 illustrates the two best angles for this kind of return. These are also the best angles to use when attempting a back wall return with your weak hand. These returns will not only force your opponent out of the front court, but might also cause him to attempt his return with his weak hand from the back left corner.

As with any good defensive shot or well-angled passing shot, these weak hand returns allow you time to move up to the all-important front court position while your opponent is retreating to the rear. Without good weak hand defensive shots, you will give your opponent setups and you will rarely have time to assume good court position before he hits his shot.

SHOT ANTICIPATION

Handball has been best described as *a constant struggle for position.* The position you take when your opponent is hitting the ball is important if you hope to have an opportunity to get into good position for your return. The ability to anticipate your opponent's shots is therefore one of handball's most important skills.

Figure 7.9 Two best shots to attempt (for righthanded players) from the rear court with the weak arm: Note that the angles are identical to those for a straight pass and two-wall pass.

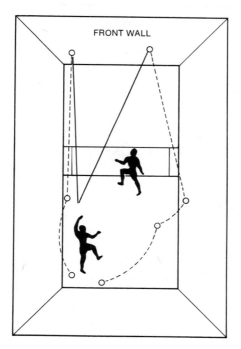

FRONT WALL

The court position you take when your opponent is hitting the ball depends on your opponent's court position and the height at which he is attempting his shot. Your ideal position when your opponent is hitting his shot is in the center of the court and a step behind the short line. (See Fig. 7.10.) This does not mean that you should run to that position after you hit every shot, but you should move toward that position while you are watching the ball and your opponent.

Watching the ball is important in shot anticipation. *Never take your eyes off of the ball.* It's easy to watch your opponent hitting the ball when he is in front of or to either side of you, but when he is attempting his shot from behind you, you must take some precautions when looking back. The chances are slim that you would ever be hit in the eye with the handball, but there is a chance; therefore, when looking back, raise your

Figure 7.10   Ideal defense court position when opponent is hitting the ball.

arm in one of the two methods demonstrated in Figure 7.11. This way you can watch the ball and have your eyes protected. Special handball eye guards are available if you feel the need for further protection. (See Fig. 7.12.) If you do not watch the ball and your opponent until he contacts his shot, you will rarely be in a good position for a fly kill or fly pass attempt, and you should always watch for the opportunity to hit these shots.

The way your opponent's feet are lined up when he hits his shot is a good indication of the direction of his return. A straight line drawn from his rear foot to his front foot as he is striding into his shot will usually be the ball's line of flight. The speed of your opponent's arm stroke will indicate how much and how fast of a rebound to expect. The height of his arm stroke is also important. If you see him attempting a shot from a high position, retreat to a court position about 8' behind the short line in order to anticipate a high return such as a ceiling shot. If your opponent's shot

Figure 7.11 Player protecting eyes while looking back at opponent: Note (a) player looks back under his raised arm, and (b) he looks back through spread fingers.

Figure 7.12 The special handball eye guard (available through the USHA).

attempt is from a low height, stay close to the short line, anticipating a kill shot but also being alert for a pass shot.

Don't ever commit yourself at full speed until your opponent has hit his shot; if his shot did not go exactly where you anticipated, you would not be able to change directions in time. However, do not be standing still when he is hitting his shot. Position your feet parallel to the front wall and be on the forward part of your feet, not on your heels. Take a step to one side or the other just as your opponent is contacting his shot—not a long stride or a crossover step, but simply a short step of about 6″ either with your right foot toward the right side wall or with your left foot toward the left side wall. This will assure that you are on your toes and ready to move. Even if the ball is hit in the opposite direction from the direction of your short step, you can change directions and get into position faster than if you had started from a complete stop. This anticipatory movement is especially important whenever it appears your opponent is attempting an offensive shot.

On deep court returns you will have more time to get into position for your attempt, but do not get to the shot just in time to make your hit. Rather, if you see your opponent is hitting a ceiling shot, move to the back wall as quickly as possible. Touch the back wall with your hand to be certain of your position (remember to keep your eyes on the ball), and then step into your shot. One of the most common mistakes in returning a high deep court shot is hitting the ball while moving backward. You should stride toward the front wall whenever you have time to do so, and good anticipation will give you this time on most shots.

Beginners often also make the mistake of moving directly toward balls that are in front court and attempting their shots from a poor position facing the front wall. If time permits, move a couple of feet to one side of the ball or the other so you will be able to turn and face a side wall when attempting your hit. Position is the most important thing in handball. If you are not in a position to take your natural arm stroke, you will not hit the ball where you want it, if indeed you hit it at all.

Get into position for your shot attempt as fast as possible so that you can come to a complete stop before striding into your shot. You should stop a few feet further from the front wall than the position from which you intend to hit your shot. This will force you to step into your shot attempt instead of hitting the ball while standing flatfooted or leaning backward. When you stop, you also have time to choose a shot to attempt in terms of your position and that of your opponent.

Analyze your opponent's pattern of play. Where does he usually hit shots in particular situations? It is very discouraging to a player who thinks he has a ball put away to see you move easily a few steps and make an effective return because you knew all along where he was going to hit and got a head start in that direction. A player usually has two or three good choices for a shot return, but many players have difficulty making certain shots. Find out the shots your opponent cannot execute well and you can better anticipate the shots he most often uses.

Never stand directly in front of or directly behind your opponent when he is hitting the ball. It's difficult to watch the ball when it is straight behind you. Always position yourself at an angle so that you can look over your shoulder to watch the ball and your opponent. If your opponent is in rear court and it appears that he is attempting an offensive shot, assume a position near the short line and directly between him and a front corner of the court. (See Fig. 7.13.)

When you make the mistake of giving your opponent a shot in the middle of the rear court, you must move out of his way, but you don't have to move far. If you are right-handed, position yourself between him and the front left corner (see Fig. 7.14); if you are left-handed, position yourself between him and the front right corner. You must give up more court than you would like, but at least he will have to attempt his shot to your strong side if he takes advantage of the opening, and you have a better chance of moving a greater distance and making an effective return with your strong hand.

Figure 7.13   Player in ideal center court position to watch his opponent in rear court.

Figure 7.14 Player hitting ball from center rear court: Note that player anticipates shot, and is just to the left of center court to not be directly in front of his opponent.

If your opponent is to the left or right side of the front court when attempting his shot, position yourself in the center of the court just behind the short line. If he is attempting his shot from the center of the front court, remember, do not stand directly behind him because you will not be able to see the ball clearly no matter where it is hit. If you are right-handed, position yourself just to his left and as close to him as possible without interfering with his swing, as illustrated in Figure 7.15. You will be able to see all of the front wall clearly, and if you lose sight of the ball after it leaves his hand, it will be angled to the side opposite him and you should quickly move in that direction.

Your particular strategy is affected by your skill and the skill of your opponent. Play according to your ability, and make the most effective use of what you have. For example, a player with great stamina can play a more defensive game. He should try to wear down his opponent with well-placed passing shots and good ceiling shots. A player with less stamina needs to hit his best serve and try to use a fly kill or fly pass in

Figure 7.15 Correct position when opponent attempts shot in front court.

order to end the rally quickly, because the longer the ball is in play the worse off he is.

Each time you play a match, have a game plan built around your strengths and your opponent's weaknesses, and try to force your opponent to play your game. Do not change a winning style, but be prepared to change your style of play if you are losing. You have nothing further to lose by trying other tactics, and you might find the answer to his game.

Paul Perlman wrote on the psychology of handball,

> *Psychology in winning handball means the ability to THINK while you play. Knowing what to do with each shot is more important than trying to blast an opponent out of the court. Once you learn to think in action you will open up an entirely new field of exercise and enjoyment. You will have greater respect for the player who "gives lessons" to mechanical marvels with million dollar hands and ten cent heads.**

*From *"ACE" Handball Magazine*, Vol. 20, No. 1 (Feb., 1970), p. 13.

Points to Remember

1. Mix up the speed, height, and direction of your serves.
2. Have a purpose for each shot you attempt.
3. Move your opponent out of front court on your service return.
4. Keep all shots and serves from coming off the back wall.
5. Always watch for the opportunity to attempt a fly kill or fly pass.
6. Know when to attempt an offensive shot and when to hit a defensive shot.
7. When you don't have a good chance to hit an offensive shot, don't hit the front wall first.
8. Use your strong hand whenever you have time and room.
9. Always watch the ball.
10. Strive for good position both when you are hitting the ball and when it is your opponent's turn to hit the ball.
11. Don't stand flatfooted when your opponent is hitting his shot.
12. Keep your opponent moving and guessing. Don't let him overanticipate your shots.
13. Play according to your ability.
14. Don't change a winning style.
15. Don't let up. Keep the pressure on.

Doubles Strategy

Teamwork is all-important when playing doubles. When it is your team's turn to make the return, which player should attempt the shot? In order to decide this, you must divide the court so that each player knows the part of the court for which he is responsible.

There are several acceptable ways to divide the court, but the method used by most championship doubles teams is shown in Figure 8.1. This assumes that both players are right-handed. Notice that the line from the front wall to the short line is down the center of the court. From the short line to the back wall the line veers slightly to the right and then goes straight to the back wall. The partner covering that territory to the right of this line is called the *right side player.* He has responsibility for the right half of the front court and the right one-third of the rear court. *The left side player* must cover the left half of the front court and the left two-thirds of the rear court.

The only difference between dividing the court in this manner and dividing the court all the way down the center from the front wall to the back wall is the small alley just to the right of center in the rear court. This alley, approximately 3' wide, is assigned to the left side player because it is easier for him to step

Figure 8.1 Court division for doubles team when both players are right-handed.

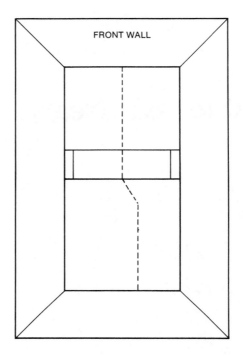

over and take the shots in this area with his strong right hand than it is for his partner to either take the shots with his left hand or back out of his good court position in order to use his right hand. If a player moves into his partner's territory to attempt a shot, there will be confusion and a part of the court will be left unprotected.

A good singles player isn't always a good doubles player. Two strong singles players can be beaten by two players of lesser individual ability with superior teamwork. A singles player must play every shot, but a doubles player doesn't necessarily hit every ball, even though it may be within his reach. Instead, he must decide whether he or his partner has the better opportunity to make a good shot. If the partner with the better shot opportunity makes the return in every case, your team is probably playing good doubles.

Playing the right side on a doubles team is quite different from playing the left side. Let us discuss each player's responsibility.

RIGHT SIDE PLAYER

It is more difficult to be a good right side player than it is to be a good left side player—not physically, but mentally. The right side player makes only about 15-20 per cent of his team's shots, and yet he must be prepared for every shot. Staying alert and taking a good court position on every shot is not easy, especially when a player knows that most of the shots will not be directed at him. It is also difficult for a right side player to let his partner return shots that he could have played. On many shots he must make the instant decision, "Should I take this shot, or, if I let it go, will my partner have a better shot?" The aim is not simply to return a shot, but to make the strongest possible return on all shots.

The right side player is generally considered the "up" man, which means that he usually positions himself closer to the front wall than does his partner. This is true especially if his opponent is attempting a shot from a low position. This would indicate a possible kill shot, in which case the right side player must move up to a position close to the short line so that he can **dig** the shot. The court position he should assume is shown in Figure 8.2. Notice that he is very close to the imaginary dividing line. He can thus attempt all his shots with his right hand.

When you play the right side of the court, don't make the mistake of positioning yourself too close to the right side wall. This would force you to play many shots with your weak left hand (assuming you are right-handed). If your opponent's shot rebounds toward your left hand, take a step toward the right wall and let your partner attempt that shot with his strong right hand.

If you see that your opponent is going to make a high return—perhaps a ceiling shot—drop back to a position about 6' behind the short line and be ready to retreat quickly even further if the shot is angled toward the right rear corner. Again, your position should be near the imaginary division line, as illustrated in Figure 8.3. From this position you will be able to make all of your deep court returns with your right hand. If your opponents' return is directed toward your left side partner, move up to a position just behind the short line, making certain that you are not in the path of your partner's return shot.

You must be constantly on the move when playing doubles. Always seek the proper court position dictated by your opponent's attempted return. Be sure to stay out of your partner's way, and move out of your opponents' way when it is their turn to make the shot. Remember that your opponent is trying to position himself very near your own ideal position, so you must watch him as well as the ball. When it is his turn to

Figure 8.2 Position of right side player (X) when opponent is attempting a low shot.

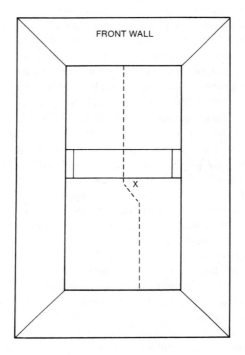

make the shot, he will usually move straight back for a deep shot or directly forward for a front court shot, and if you are in his path you should move in a semicircle to get out of his way and to get to your proper court position. (See Fig. 8.4.)

When your right side opponent is attempting a shot from back court, do not position yourself directly in front of him. Always try to assume a position at a slight angle from him so you can look back over one shoulder and watch him. If your right side opponent is attempting a shot in front court, do not position yourself directly behind him. You will not be able to see his shot when it hits the front wall. Rather, position yourself slightly behind and to one side of him.

Your best position is near the imaginary division line, but you cannot always be in that position. If your opponent is in that area to attempt his shot, you must move over toward the right side wall to allow him room. Your team has obviously made a poor shot if your opponent

Figure 8.3 Position of right side player (X) when opponent is attempting a high return.

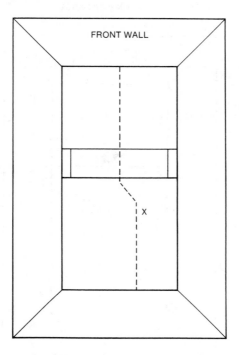

has a shot from a part of the court which forces you out of your ideal court position.

If your opponent attempts a low shot, your position is normally up close to the short line. However, if the shot is angled toward your left side partner and he must move into the left front court to attempt his shot, you should quickly retreat a few steps so that you will be in position to return any deep court shot in case your partner isn't able to recover in time. Thus, one player should usually have a slightly deeper court position than his partner. In case a shot is driven past the man playing closest to the front wall, his partner can move over and make the return.

THE LEFT SIDE PLAYER

The left side doubles player is definitely the workhorse of the team. Most of the shots are played by him, and because of this, he should have

Figure 8.4   Semicircular movement to get into good position for right side player (X): Note that this must be done without interfering with opponent (O) moving to play the shot.

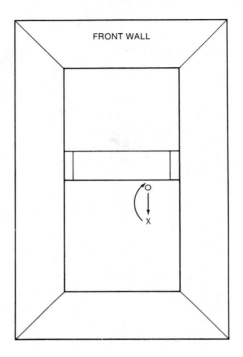

good endurance and possess a good left hand as well as a good right. He is much like a singles player because he plays most of the shots, and he should even move toward shots that are angled toward his right side partner. If he sees that his partner is going to make the return, he can move back to his normal court position. But should a shot get by his partner, he will then have a good chance to make the return.

The left side player's ideal court position is shown in Figure 8.5. Notice that he is a few feet behind the short line and a couple of steps from the left side wall. Although he will be in many different court positions to attempt his returns, this is the position he should move toward after having hit his shot. He may move a step closer to the front wall if his opponent is attempting a low shot, and he should retreat a couple of steps if it appears that his opponent is going to return the ball

Figure 8.5 Ideal position of right-handed left side player (X).

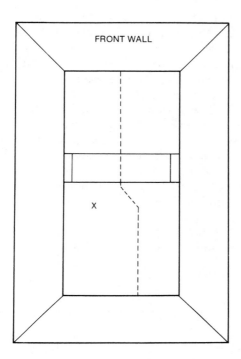

into deep court. If he must move into the front court to make his return, he should try to move back quickly to his normal position. His left hand is vulnerable when he is too close to the front wall. A hard driven shot from his opponent might get by his left hand and force his partner out of position to attempt the return.

When the opponent's shot is rebounding down the center of the court, the left side player must move toward and play this shot so that his partner will not be forced to attempt a left-handed return.

The left side player's position is usually deeper in the court than the position of his partner, and he can best determine who should play the shots that are close to the imaginary division line. The left side player should call the shot by shouting *"mine"* or *"yours."* These two words are short and easily understood and should be the only words said while the rally is in progress.

THE LEFT-HANDED PARTNER

When one of the partners is left-handed, the court division is slightly different than it is for two right-handed players. Figure 8.6 illustrates this court division down the middle of the court from the front wall to the back wall. The left-handed partner should position himself close to the imaginary division line, as was discussed earlier.

The weakness of a doubles team with one left-handed and one right-handed partner is on shots rebounding down the middle of the court. Who should attempt to return these shots? This decision should be made before the game starts. The partner who possesses the stronger off-hand should be the one to play the shots rebounding into this weak territory. If the two partners' off-hands are about equal, the player who is in the best position for the shot should attempt the return. Usually this is a problem only on shots in the front court. If a ball is hit down the middle into the

Figure 8.6 Court division for right-handed—left-handed doubles team.

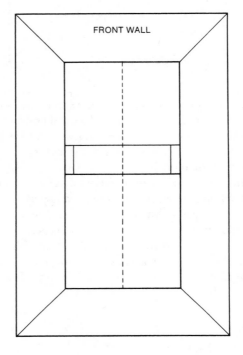

FRONT WALL

rear court, one partner will probably have time to move around the shot and make the return with his dominant hand.

Because such a team's weakness is down the middle of the court, the left-handed player's ideal court position is closer to the imaginary division line than the position taken by a left side player who is right-handed. (See Fig. 8.7.) The team's weak area will thus be smaller, and the left-handed player will be able to hit more shots with his dominant left hand. Shots angled toward this team's weak area will cause confusion as to which player should attempt the return unless the players quickly call "mine" or "yours"—a call that must be made for all shots hit down the middle of the court.

RETURN OF SERVICE

As in singles, a good return of service is very important. The position for each partner when receiving a serve is illustrated in Figure 8.8. If the

Figure 8.7 Ideal position of left-handed left side player.

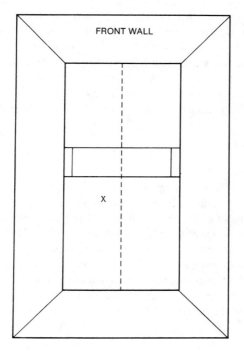

Figure 8.8   (a) Position of right-handed doubles team to receive serve. (b) Position of team to receive serve when left side player is left-handed.

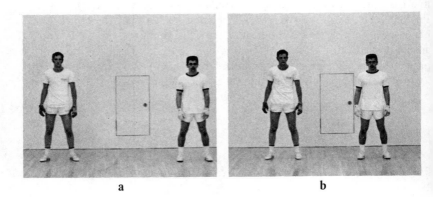

a   b

team has a left-handed player and a right-handed player, each player should position himself about one foot closer to the center so that the weak area between them will be smaller. Should the serve result in a setup, the man playing the shot should attempt one of the offensive kill or pass shots. If the serve is too difficult for the player to attempt an offensive shot, he should return a ceiling shot or a three-wall return in order to move the opponents into a rear court position. The player not returning the serve should quickly move up close to the short line as his partner is making the return, making sure he will not be in the path of the ball.

THE SERVE

The most effective serve in doubles is one directed toward the weakness of the opposing team. Some experimenting with your good serves is necessary in order to determine where that weakness lies. If your opponents are both right-handed, you will usually find it better to serve to the left hand of the left side player. A serve directed anywhere else can be returned by the dominant right hand of one of the players. You can attempt any of the serves that were discussed in Chapter 5.

If your opponents are left-handed and right-handed, your serves should be directed down the middle, toward their off-hands. You can serve a straight low drive serve to this area or a low drive serve that hits the side wall just behind the short line and will then angle to the middle of the rear court. (See Fig. 8.9.)

The right side player should stand somewhere between the center of the court and the right side wall when attempting his serve. If he stands to the left of center he may be caught out of position when his opponent makes the return shot. The left side player should stand between the middle of the court and the left side wall when serving, for the same reason.

In order to assume good court position quickly following the serve, the right side player should stand in the right doubles box when his partner is serving, and the left side player should stand in the left doubles box when his partner is serving.

Figure 8.9 A low drive angle serve that rebounds between receivers: Note that this is a good serve to use against a left-handed—right-handed doubles team.

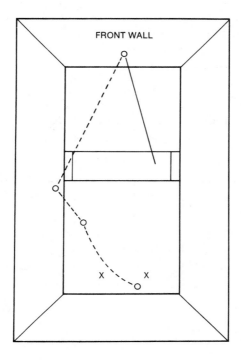

STRATEGY AFTER THE SERVE

The most effective offensive shot in doubles is the kill shot. A passing shot is difficult to hit when your opponents are in good court position, although if both of your opponents make the mistake of being too close to the front wall, a two-wall pass shot is effective. However, most of the time one opponent is positioned deeper than his partner, and in order to win the rally a kill shot must be used.

The best strategy in doubles is to try to move one of your opponents into a rear court position and then shoot for a kill shot that will end up in the front half of the court for which he is responsible. A fly kill shot is especially important because it doesn't allow your opponent time to regain his good court position. Figure 8.10 illustrates the best kill shots to

Figure 8.10   Best kill shots to attempt when right side opponent (X_2) is in deep court: Note that the shots rebound to front right court.

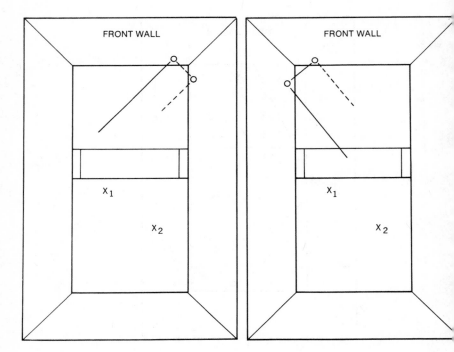

attempt if the right side opponent is caught in deep court, and Figure 8.11 shows the best choice of kill shots if the left side opponent's position is deep. Directing your kill shots to the proper place will allow you to end the rally without having to execute a perfect rollout kill shot.

Doubles differs from singles in that all shots should be hit hard. (The exception is the ceiling shot which is never hit hard.) It is nearly impossible to hit a soft shot that one of your opponents cannot reach. Hit your kill shots with power, and if they are not perfect, at least your opponent will not have time to set and attempt a rekill. The hard, driving three-wall return shot is a very effective doubles shot that quite often confuses your opponents as to which of them should attempt the return.

If you don't have a good opportunity to execute a kill shot, direct your shot toward your opponents' weakness. Against two right-handed opponents, hit driving pass shots down the left wall or ceiling shots angled

Figure 8.11 Best kill shots to attempt when left side opponent (X_1) is in deep court: Note that shots rebound to front left court.

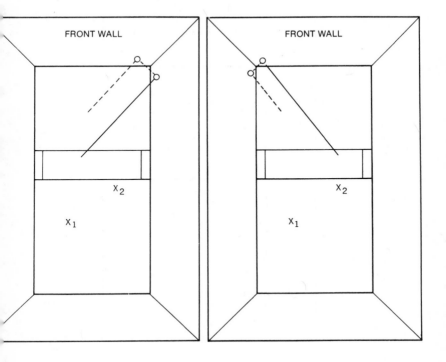

into the left rear corner in order to force a return with the player's off-hand which might result in a setup for your team.

Against left-handed and right-handed players, the three-wall return is an especially good shot because the ball angles through the center of the court on its rebound. If you must hit the front wall first with your return, a good shot is one that hits the front wall close to a front corner so that it then strikes the side wall and rebounds diagonally across the center of the court. (See Fig. 8.12.) A ceiling shot might be a good shot, but it is impossible to force a weak hand return from a left-handed—right-handed team with any ceiling shot. One of the opponents can make a dominant hand return on any ceiling shot.

Another type of strategy to use against a doubles team is to **freeze out** one of your opponents. Find out if one player can beat two. Serve every serve to that player, and direct every shot to him during the rally.

Figure 8.12 Good angle shot to use against a left-handed—right-handed doubles team: Note that ball rebounds to team's weakness.

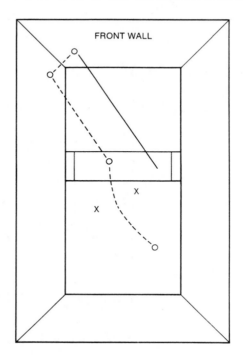

Not only might you tire him, but his partner will be cold and unlikely to hit a good shot should you accidentally hit a shot his direction. This method can be very effective and should be tried any time you think your opponents are superior to you and your partner.

Much practice is necessary to develop good teamwork. Knowing your partner's moves and favorite shots in particular situations will enable you to take a position in the court to the best advantage. You and your partner must both concentrate your shots toward your opponents' weakness, so if you spot a weakness, let your partner know about it.

It is very important to offer encouragement to your partner, even if he happens to be playing poorly.

Points to Remember

1. Just because the ball is within your reach does not mean you should attempt the shot. Perhaps your partner has the opportunity for a better shot.
2. When two right-handed players are playing together, the right side player should rarely attempt a shot with his left hand.
3. Don't get trapped too near the side walls.
4. Always watch the ball.
5. Know the position of each opponent so you can choose the correct shot to attempt.
6. Try not to position yourself directly in front of or directly behind your opponent.
7. The kill shot is the primary offensive shot in doubles.
8. The weak area of a left-handed—right-handed team is down the center of the court.
9. If you cannot attempt a kill shot, drive the ball hard toward your opponents' weak area or hit a soft ceiling shot into one of the rear corners.
10. Call "mine" or "yours" for shots when there is some doubt as to which player should play the shot.

Etiquette

Handball, like all sports, has many unwritten rules as well as written ones. These unwritten rules have to do with the sportsmanlike behavior and courteous manners that contribute to the enjoyment of the game by players and spectators alike. This chapter provides a brief summary of handball etiquette.

If you set up a match at a particular time, be suited out and ready to go on time. If you do not have a game and you are at the courts looking for someone to play, try to find players with approximately your own skill. Games with players whose skills are far apart are often unenjoyable for both players.

Wear the proper uniform and wear a clean uniform. If it is a warm day, take along an extra T-shirt to change into when the one you are wearing gets so wet that perspiration dripping on the floor is creating a safety hazard. Take a towel so you can dry your face from time to time or dry the floor if it gets wet. Have at least two pairs of gloves with you in case one pair begins to get wet. It is an unfair advantage to play with wet gloves because the ball gets wet when you strike it, which causes it to take abnormal bounces.

Do not rush your opponent. Give him ample time to warm up before beginning the game. Before serving, always look back to your opponent to be sure he is set and ready.

Never stamp your feet to distract your opponent as he is about to attempt his shot. Handball requires intense concentration, and a player should not be distracted by unnecessary noise. Do not talk while the ball is in play. The only exception is in doubles, when it is permissible for partners to call "mine" or "yours." Spectators should also refrain from talking or applauding while the rally is in progress. However, after the rally is over, the spectators may applaud as they see fit, and a player should not hestitate to compliment his opponent on a particularly good shot.

In a tournament match, a referee decides all questions that arise during play, and a scorekeeper keeps the players informed of the score after every rally. Most of the games you play will not be tournament matches. Therefore, you and your opponent have the responsibility for deciding questionable plays and for keeping the score. If you disagree with your opponent about the legitimacy of a play, replay the point. Accept your opponent's judgment when he calls shorts or hinders. *Nothing takes the fun out of a contest any faster than an argument between players.*

Sometimes only the player attempting the shot knows whether or not he has made a legal return. If you make an illegal return by hitting the ball on the second bounce or by hitting the ball on your wrist, you should say so. Calls on yourself should also be made in tournament matches, because the referee often cannot see these illegal plays.

Any time the ball hits a player it should be checked for wet spots and dried off. Let your opponent also check the ball to see if it meets his satisfaction before putting it back into play. When returning the ball to your opponent after a rally, bounce the ball to him Injuries have resulted from balls being thrown to the server. Do not hit the ball after the rally is over. It can be dangerous to the other players in the court.

Call out the score at the end of each rally and before serving. Call the server's score first.

Most questionable plays that arise during a game have to do with hinders. *Review Rules 4.10 and 4.11 on hinders.* It is your duty to move out of your opponent's way so he has a fair chance to play the ball, even if it means that you must give up your good court position. Call a hinder only when you are certain that if your opponent had not been in your way, you could have reached the ball in time to make a legal return. Just because your opponent is between you and the ball does not mean it is a hinder.

Try your best to avoid body contact with your opponent. Never push or shove your opponent in your attempt to make a return. If you see you will have to contact him in order to play the ball, stop and call a hinder instead.

Do not take option shots. On close plays in which a hinder might be called, don't attempt your shot and then call a hinder if you miss the shot. The player playing the ball should call the hinder. If, however, he does not see the ball clearly enough to be sure of the call, he should ask his opponent if he thought the ball was playable and accept his opponent's judgment on the call.

If you are playing a friendly doubles game, alternate your serves first to one opponent and then the other. Never criticize or get angry with your doubles partner.

Be a good winner as well as a gracious loser. If you lose, congratulate your opponent on his victory and don't make excuses for your defeat.

Play hard to win, play fairly, and enjoy the contest.

Suggested Readings

BOOKS

O'Connell, Charlie, *Handball Illustrated.* New York: The Ronald Press Company, 1964.

Phillips, B.E., *Handball: Its Play and Management.* New York: The Ronald Press Company, 1957.

Plotnicki, Ben A., and Andrew J. Kozar, *Handball.* Dubuque, Iowa: Kendall/Hunt Publishing Company, 1970.

Roberson, Richard, and Herbert Olson, *Beginning Handball.* Belmont, California: Wadsworth Publishing Company, Inc., 1962.

Tunis, John R., *Sport for the Fun of It.* New York: A.S. Barnes and Company, 1940.

Yessis, Michael, *Handball.* Dubuque, Iowa: Wm. C. Brown Company, Publishers, 1966.

MAGAZINES

Ace Handball Magazine (Official Publication of The United States Handball Association, 4101 Dempster Street, Skokie, Illinois).